Total Package Girl
Discover the Ultimate You For Life!

Cora,
Stay strong and
courageous ... #jbu ...

Kristi K. Hoffman

authorHOUSE®

AuthorHouse™
1663 Liberty Drive
Bloomington, IN 47403
www.authorhouse.com
Phone: 1 (800) 839-8640

Published by AuthorHouse   04/06/2016

ISBN: 978-1-5049-2731-4 (sc)
ISBN: 978-1-5049-2730-7 (hc)
ISBN: 978-1-5049-2729-1 (e)

Library of Congress Control Number: 2015912585

Print information available on the last page.

This book is printed on acid-free paper.

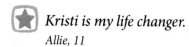

Rockin' *Total Package Girl Quotes*

⭐ *Kristi is my life changer.*
Allie, 11

⭐ ***Total Package Girl*** *taught me who I am and how to be myself ... for life.*
Sarah, 13

⭐ ***Total Package Girl*** *made me feel proud to be me and taught me that I have so much potential.*
Jamie, 12

⭐ ***Total Package Girl*** *taught me how to be confident.*
Lily, 13

⭐ ***Total Package Girl*** *taught me how to just be me, no matter what I look like ... or what others think.*
Julia, 14

⭐ ***Total Package Girl*** *taught me how to be strong, to love me, and to rock my own power!*
Anonymous, 16

⭐ *The most valuable lesson this book taught me was to be me and embrace myself.*
Hailey, 13

⭐ *As a parent and an educator raising a girl in the 21st century, I highly recommend **Total Package Girl** as a resource to help guide any daughter to become a confident and successful young woman who is proud of her past, present, and future decisions.*
Scott, Father of 3

Total Package Girl has been described by girls, teachers, mothers, fathers, and grandparents as:

TOTAL PACKAGE

Girl

DISCOVER THE

Ultimate You

FOR Life!

KRISTI K. HOFFMAN

To Brett and Drew—
my incredible sources of
inspiration and love.
I am truly blessed.

CONTENTS

PART I

Meet the Unstoppable Total Package Girl   1

PART IV

Be the Total Package Girl for Life

About this Book and the Author

Total Package Girl is not a parenting book. It is a book written for girls. Kristi K. Hoffman was once a young girl with an unstoppable passion. Today that passion continues.

Kristi has been an award-winning TV host and producer, businesswoman, mom, wife, sister, friend, daughter, and volunteer. She has had a life filled with rich blessings and experiences. Kristi wrote *Total Package Girl* using miles of life footprints. Through this book as well as her keynote speeches and workshops, she shares her knowledge and experience, as well as her savvy life lessons, with girls across the globe. One of Kristi's life goals is to help girls, boys, young professionals, and executives be strong and powerful in their lives.

Beginning when she was young, through her junior-high and high-school years, her undergraduate and graduate-school days, and her career and volunteer experiences, Kristi has passionately observed and journaled life lessons. Working in television—on air—reinforced the value of having a positive body image for life. Coordinating a regional effort in the first-ever "Take Our Daughters to Work Day" in the early 1990s (since expanded to include boys), revealed the excitement on girls' faces as they lived out their career aspirations, and led Kristi down the path of mentoring and eventually developing Total Package Global. Kristi's passion for "knowledge transfer" to future generations became unstoppable.

Kristi's compelling writing reveals deep power, strength, and knowledge. She has learned that positive action speaks volumes. That some words are better left unspoken. That mistakes happen—learn from them. That it's great to be an individual. That true friends come in all shapes and sizes. That life's "right now" moments, good health, and the precious human spirit are to be cherished, loved, and celebrated.

Throughout her twenty-five years of professional and volunteer experience and her hundreds of interviews with corporate executives, CEOs, entrepreneurs, professional and collegiate athletes, and young girls and boys, Kristi has gleaned notable and life-altering lessons. Her affiliations with such organizations as Boston University, PBS, CBS, Girl Scouts of the USA, Young Presidents' Organization (YPO), World Presidents' Organization (WPO), University of Toledo, Junior League, and Delta Delta Delta sorority have made her who she is today. Kristi is not a psychologist or a medical doctor, nor does she profess to be one. She is, however, personally dedicated to living the Total Package Lifestyle—a commitment to being fit, healthy, and energetic in Body, Brain, and Spirit.

The underlying approach of *Total Package Girl* is both academic and experiential. It includes a-ha moments, thought-driven messages, inspirational quotes, and deep-dive activities, so girls may discover their *total package* of Body, Brain and Spirit. *Total Package Girl* acknowledges that falling down is a part of life, yet the Total Package Lifestyle is about getting up, forgiving oneself and others, finding personal power and confidence, and discovering the ultimate, amazing *you* inside and out.

So girls ... this is a book written for you. It is not meant to be a parenting book, but if your parents want to read it with you and are compelled to use it as reinforcement or a resource, so much the better! Feel free to bring them into the Total Package Girl world.

Total Package Girl is a guide to help you love yourself, be positive, feel strong and powerful, and stay on a fit, healthy, energetic, and fun path—the Total Package Lifestyle! Through this book, Kristi hopes that every single girl will respect and love herself; turn away from negativity and poor influences; walk with confidence, kindness, and clear direction; and ultimately reach her dreams. Kristi hopes *Total Package Girl* will help you be more grounded and centered in totality, live true to yourself, be kind and deeply loving, be savvy in your choices, and have fun doing it!

Kristi's Total Package Global, a professional and personal development corporation, has the mission of energizing and developing savvy, real, and successful individuals across the globe, inside and out, at work and in life. Among other things, Total Package Global offers lifestyle tools to assist people in setting and reaching their success goals and dreams. Kristi herself has learned to blend her talents with her loves to create a fulfilled and blessed life. She developed the Total Package Lifestyle to help people live a fit, healthy, centered, and energetic life.

Welcome to your new Total Package Girl life. Seize the **right now** moment, girls!

For Kristi's detailed biography, go to:
www.TotalPackageGirl.com/CEO

Preface

Total Package Girl is for every girl who is figuring it out, finding herself, living through the challenges of growing up, and discovering how truly amazing she is.

The goal of this book is to enlighten you about the secret weapons successful girls and young women know—and to teach you how to use them. *Total Package Girl* aims to guide you on your life path. When life gets bumpy, when the path in front of you gets tricky, or when you're facing a huge fork in the road, *Total Package Girl* is here for you, providing intelligence and insight, ideas and consultation, relateability and energy. It's real. It's heartfelt. It's for you. Consider this book your personal BFF.

Throughout *Total Package Girl*, you will learn how to build:

 Confidence, knowledge, and trust in yourself

 A healthy, rockin' body image

 Awesome communication skills

 Your own success strategy for living your dreams

This book is about living the Total Package Lifestyle—one of always going back to your core, of staying true to you, of navigating or steering clear of the negatives that life throws your way. Be committed to the intelligence in this book, stay the course, and trust that it works. Thousands know it does.

Acknowledgments

Total Package Girl has been an evolution—my evolution. In many ways, you could say I've spent my entire life writing this book, growing up as a young Midwestern girl, until today. Yet specifically and deliberately, I've spent the past ten years researching, interviewing, and speaking with thousands to develop its contents.

The goal of *Total Package Girl* is to blend qualitative and quantitative research with professional and personal experiences to create the best possible intelligence guide for each and every girl seeking to be stronger, more grounded, and more amazing than she already is.

For those who have helped me throughout the *Total Package Girl* process, I thank you. Categorically, you are:

Seed planters

You've helped me discover, develop, and blend my talents and my loves. You've valued my opinions. You've taught me life lessons and led me down positive paths. You've steered me away from negative influences and poorly conceived ideas, and you've been ever-patient, willing, and open-minded. You've talked me through the book, the business, the strategy, the direction, the path. You've never questioned my unstoppable desire to be more, do more, help more. I'm eternally grateful for your influence, patience, and direction.

Seed waterers

You've helped me keep the process moving steadily forward, advancing my mission and helping me grow. You've not hesitated to open a door, make a connection, or offer your expertise. You've provided insight and knowledge that I didn't previously have. I'm grateful for your motivation, your confidence in me, your brilliance, and your willingness to help, no questions asked.

TruBlues

You've been there with me, never leaving my side, during the victories and the challenges. You've stayed close and didn't run the other way. You've shown and taught me what unconditional love truly is. You've kept—and continue to keep—me grounded, positive, and excited about life. You've listened without judgment and have offered support when needed; I didn't have to ask. You continue to be the brightest stars, my rays of sunshine. You've run, walked, and crawled beside me. I am grateful for your unconditional love, your steadfastness, your soul.

Inspirations

Like trailblazers, you've gone before me. You've made me want to be a stronger, smarter, and more awesome human being. You've expanded my limits and have taught me to reach out when I have wanted to cower. You've brought a spark of inspiration, rich learning moments, laughter, and unbelievable memories into my world. You've shown by example the value of excellence, bravery, power, and foresight. I am grateful for your strength, your compassion, your intelligence, and the brave steps you took.

Character builders

You've done or said something that has influenced my life positively or negatively. Your positive words may have pushed and encouraged me to take a different, more assertive path than I would have taken without them. Conversely, you may have provided me with an example of how not to be or what not to do, and through your negative words or actions, you've taught me to be better, stronger, braver. Thank you for the life lessons, for building my character, and for strengthening my spirit. You've helped shape me on the potter's wheel. Most of all, thank you for instilling in me exactly what I needed to write this book: *Courage.*

On a long journey like this, one's soul is exposed and one's spirit is revealed. People come and go. Experiences are rich and evolving. Valuable encounters leave indelible marks—the footprints of our lives. I am grateful for my seed planters, seed waterers, TruBlues, inspirations, and character builders:

God—with You, all things are possible.

Jim—you've walked beside me, helping me achieve and live my dreams.

Brett and Drew—I love you unconditionally … you amaze and inspire me.

Mom and Dad—you've planted and watered the seeds, giving me roots, sacrificing, and providing love always.

Karen—you've been there through it all—the laughter and the tears—with support and love the whole time.

Norma—you've passed on your incredible wisdom and love.

Beloved family—for your faith, love, and kindness including: Kathy, Ben, Nick, Christian, my fabulous nephews and nieces, and those who offer caring support.

Susan Frantz—for your amazing expertise, patience, and unending support in laying out, editing, and completing this book with me.

Kristy, Jenny, and Gerina—you are my amazing, loving, beautiful LPGA daughters.

Others who've truly made a difference: Roni Luckenbill— CEO, Girl Scouts of Western Ohio; Cynthia Thompson— brilliant mentor and former board president, Girl Scouts of the USA; Tom Beaty—the most supportive, encouraging, honest boss ever; Linda Karazim, PhD, and Ethel Wilcox, PhD—for teaching me well; Miss Hathaway— for recognizing my talents; Roxanne Sukol, MD and Cleveland Clinic Foundation—for the invaluable medical expertise; Dr. Jauregui—for saving my life. Thank you Margaret Beck, JD; Tom Fiedler, Dean, Boston University College of Communication; Girl Scouts of Western Ohio, and Girl Scouts of the USA.

To Grandma H., Grandma and Grandpa P., David, Gretchen, Gloria, and other dear ones—I miss your smiles, your voices, your love, and your hugs.

To Stephanie, Allyson, MaryBeth, and Tracey—you've helped keep me grounded. To Heidi, Steve at Hanson Productions, Paula, Hilary, Christy, Allison, Veronica, Judy, and Holly— for getting and/or keeping the ball rolling.

For the Zen moments, love my Zéya and Eloise.

And to the thousands of girls who've inspired me in writing this book (you rock!)—including Emma, Priya, Maddie, Autumn, Lily, Kendall, and Carly.

Daily, I remember the blessings of good health, true friends, and unconditional love. I am grateful for life's lessons that reveal themselves, and am in awe of the beauty that exists in each and every person, if only I remember to look.

I pray that *Total Package Girl* will be your life changer, seed planter, seed waterer, character builder, and/or inspiration. For if *you*—one amazing girl reading this book—gain the courage to live the Total Package Lifestyle, I will have achieved the ultimate life success ... by my own definition.

Love, strength, and blessings,

Kristi K.

Check Out Our Hashtags

The following are hashtags used throughout this book and in social media. They represent the Total Package Girl brand and emphasize relevant phrases and terms we use to spread the word about our passion for living a fit, healthy, energetic life. Tweet and post away using our hashtags!

Introduction

To live the Total Package Girl Lifestyle, you must live in the present moment.

At first, this a tough concept to grasp. We use the term "right now" to help define it more clearly. "Right now" is used often throughout *Total Package Girl* to remind you to breathe in that exact moment, to be in the here and now, to acknowledge the precise thought you are thinking, the words you are reading, the feeling you are feeling, the specific smell you are smelling, and the vivid sights and colors you are seeing.

Being super-aware of your exact moment in time is critical to living life to its fullest, to learning all you can, to being the best you can be—with your eyes open to your surroundings, to your place in time, to your "right now" moment. As former Boston University College of Communication professor Dr. Marilyn Root would say, "Be here now." We Total Package Girls get it, Dr. Root. Thank you.

The vibrancy and energy of the "right now" moment is powerful. Feel the clarity. Absorb the smells, sights, and sounds. Embrace and live the moment.

Throughout this book, definitions of words or terms will show up between two dotted lines. Then, after the definition, you'll find an italicized sentence using that particular word or phrase in context. In the back of *Total Package Girl*, there is a glossary of all the definitions used in the book.

#RightNow (adj., adv., n.)

To be in the here and now, to acknowledge the precise thought you are thinking, the words you are reading, the feelings you are feeling, the specific smell you are smelling, and the vivid sights and colors you are seeing.

Being acutely aware of your moment in time is critical to living life to its fullest, with your eyes open to your surroundings, your place in time, your #RightNow moment.

For added motivation and wisdom, *Total Package Girl* also incorporates ribbons with some of our favorite motivational and wise quotes, such as:

#RightNow is the oldest you've ever been
and the youngest you'll ever be,
so seize this moment, be here now,
and live your Total Package Girl dreams.

PART I

Meet the Unstoppable Total Package Girl

Who Is the Total Package Girl?

Meet *her*. The #TotalPackageGirl. She has an aura, an essence, a charisma. She seems amazing in a friendly yet irresistible sort of way. Defining her is a bit of a mystery. Before you get to know her, you observe that everyone, including you, likes her and enjoys being near her, not in a "put her up on a pedestal and worship her" kind of way, but rather in a "want to be around her because she is awesome" way.

Is she perfectly perfect? Does she do everything exactly right? No. No one is and no one does. Does she make mistakes? Yes, of course. Everyone does. Yet she still seems to have it all going on. People like her—really like her—in spite of her imperfections. What a novel concept!

. . . .

Unstoppable (adj.)

Amazing, invincible, awesome, on fire; feelin' it; a force to be reckoned with, incapable of being stopped.

*#RightNow, you are becoming an amazing, savvy, **unstoppable** Total Package Girl.*

. . . .

Why all the love for this so-called Total Package Girl? On the outside, she exudes confidence. People are attracted to that energy, that smile, that package. Then when you actually talk to this Total Package Girl, you learn that she's approachable. She's nice and charismatic on the inside. One could describe the Total Package Girl as:

 Happy and confident

 Friendly, easy to talk to, genuine, and nice to everyone

 Not gossipy or someone who says bad words about another person; not two-faced

 Not boastful or trying to impress others with possessions or looks

 Hardworking, takes school seriously; a quiet leader

 Good at decision-making

 Not a stir-it-up, get-into-trouble kind of girl

For these reasons and more, she's the unstoppable Total Package Girl. She focuses on positive things like taking care of her Body, Brain, and Spirit, and she clearly has some secret weapons—things that she knows deep inside that others have yet to learn, sort of like a secret society of quietly amazing girls.

That Girl: A Story

She was a shy Midwestern girl. Perhaps attractive, but she didn't know it. Perhaps happy, but she wasn't sure. As a young girl, she often felt scared and insecure about how she looked, what she wore, what she said. Ah ... those thick glasses she'd worn since she was six didn't help; the hand-me-down clothes she often wore didn't help her confidence either. Early on, she didn't really know who she was, what she stood for, or who her true friends were.

That Girl was humble and modest. She rarely, if ever, used her voice to speak up. ("How *do* you speak up anyway?" she wondered.) She let others speak for her, telling her how she felt, making her decisions for her. She wished she knew how to take a stand, how to speak up, how to make friends more easily. Life was serious for That Girl.

That Girl wouldn't hurt a fly. If she did, it would devastate her; her intentions were pure. When she did speak, her words came out awkwardly, not how she wanted them to. Yet she spoke the truth. She didn't brag about her gifts, her academic and athletic achievements, her happy moments. She left them alone, never to be shared—just like the little victories she didn't share or the battles she fought inside. Most went unnoticed, unspoken, within her mind.

She watched the behaviors of others and learned. She heard mean girls say nasty words to those who were different than the rest. It made her sad. Mad even. She stayed away from mean girls; not her thing. Instead, she chose steady friends who also had been looking for true friends. She liked these friends for who they were, and vice versa. They made her feel good and confident about herself. They were true. It was refreshing.

She stayed quiet pretty much throughout her elementary-school years but continued watching, learning, and absorbing the behaviors and words of others, both kind and mean.

That Girl did her very best not to gossip, be rude, or exclude others. On the playground, she chose to play with those who had no one to play with rather than run with those who excluded others. ("Why are people mean?" she'd worry.) This choice felt better—more natural—to her.

Like clay being molded, That Girl was learning as she watched, as she experienced. She stayed away from trouble, stayed consistently nice. People were not always nice back, That Girl learned, nor were they always who they seemed to be. She was growing up, getting smarter, becoming savvier, making mistakes and learning from them most of the time. All the while, she was being molded into a uniquely beautiful piece of art, although she didn't know it.

Everyone finds confidence from a place deep within. Find your confidence and let it take you places you've never been before. **Relax, enjoy who you are, and just be you. #jbu**

Insight: The Total Package Girl isn't preoccupied with everyone else's status, what they're wearing, what activities they're going to join, whose house they're going to. Instead, she's running her own race and setting her own GPS in the direction of her dreams, interests, and feelings. She's real—a Total Package Girl with a focus on the positive things in life … unlike the mean girl.

Who Is the Mean Girl?

Meet *her*. The Mean Girl. She is swarming with frenemies, unclear as to what a true friend is. Quantity of friends is more important than quality when it comes to the mean girl.

Like a bee, she has a stinger—in her words and in her relationships. She's an identity thief; when others follow her, they lose who they are, trying too hard to be like her. She stirs up controversy and hurts others with her sharp tongue, her bully tactics, and her hot-and-cold attitude. Who knows how she's going to act from one day to the next? Will she like you or will she be mean and ignore you? Will you be on her good side or her bad side?

The mean girl seeks to control those who may be too timid to stand up for themselves, or who are lost or directionless and follow the mean girl around in hopes of finding a leader. Instead, these girls go deeper into the dark forest, led astray by the mean girl.

The mean girl does not ooze qualities like friendship, love, loyalty or compassion for another human being. It's all about her own interests. After all, she's the head honcho, and she uses her attitude to judge others and to intimidate and inflict the feeling of "never good enough" upon those girls falling prey.

When you talk to the mean girl (if she'll let you), you'll likely learn the following:

- *Trouble follows her.*

- *She isn't consistently nice.*

- *She may judge people on possessions, what they look like, what they wear ... nothing truly deep or relevant.*

- *She often holds "tryouts" for her friends to see who is "good enough." Those who fall in line with her way of thinking win her temporary friendship.*

- *She doesn't know who her "real" self is because she's so busy playing her stinging games.*

- *She gossips, starts rumors about others, and posts negative comments (but rarely makes them to others' faces).*

- *She gets mad easily, plays games with others' emotions, and is disrespectful to many.*

❎ *Ironically, she may be very nice at times—which is confusing to those who so desperately want to be her friend because the niceness is unpredictable and doesn't seem to last.*

These mean-girl tactics get old and exhausting really fast to those who can see right through them. Confident girls quit this game and move on, but others who haven't yet learned the courageous Total Package Girl secret weapons may struggle to get out of the negative mean-girl cycle.

CAUTIONARY NOTE!

Attaching yourself to a mean girl may result in peer-pressure trouble in the future as you find yourself in a constant "follower" or "pack" mentality. You may also be endangered by a world that relies heavily on looks, possessions, quantity of friends, and bullying tactics. Mean-girl foundations are built on sand and can crumble at any time. Stay strong and build your own rock-solid friendships and Total Package Girl foundation.

TOTAL PACKAGE GIRL ACTIVITY:
Total Package Girls and Mean Girls

Do I know a mean girl? If yes, do I try to be her friend?

☐ Yes ☒ No

If yes, why? ....

Do I know a person who likes me some days and doesn't like me other days?

☒ Yes ☐ No

Do I consider her a true friend? ☐ Yes ☒ No

Do I know a Total Package Girl? ☒ Yes ☒ No

If yes, what qualities do I enjoy most about her?

⭐ .... ⭐ ....

Do I consider her a true friend? ☐ Yes ☐ No

Why or why not? ....

Do I have Total Package Girl qualities? ☒ Yes ☐ No

If yes, what are they?

⭐ Kind ⭐ caring
⭐ don't brag ⭐ helpful

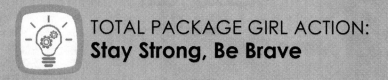

TOTAL PACKAGE GIRL ACTION:
Stay Strong, Be Brave

Hang out with people who are truly nice to you on a regular basis. Look for and see the differences between the Total Package Girl and the mean girl. When your eyes are open to these differences, have the courage to walk away from the mean girl. Choose to live a Total Package Girl life. Quality counts, not quantity.

Trying-Too-Hard Syndrome

Ever see someone who frequently changes her likes, interests, clothing, or even personality to be accepted by someone else? Perhaps it has happened to you. You may find yourself trying so very hard—even sacrificing your own beliefs, interests, and loves—just to fit in. If this happens to you, no worries. Just recognize it and realize that you may not yet have learned to stay true to yourself, which is a Total Package Girl secret weapon.

If you find yourself going to great lengths to create an artificial image of yourself just to impress others, remind yourself that this syndrome can be cured by understanding that true friends will love you for just who you are ... no need to change to fit in. **#jbu**

Pretty-Girl Syndrome

Pretty-Girl Syndrome may begin at a young age when you receive a lot of attention and repeated or excessive compliments on your looks—the physical part of you only. For example, "OMG, look how gorgeous you are" or "You are so beautiful—look at those legs" or "Your body is perfect." While it's nice to receive compliments for sure and to feel good about how you look, excessive emphasis on only the physical aspect can set up unattainable expectations of perfectionism, actually planting seeds for an unhealthy body image.

This syndrome also may offer a false sense of believing that because you are perceived as pretty, you can get whatever you want when you want it, simply by how you look. If and when actions become tied primarily to looks, it becomes difficult to learn that it's the *total package* of you—the combined Body, Brain, and Spirit—that leads to reaching your dreams, gaining success, and feeling happy within yourself. With Pretty-Girl Syndrome, you don't realize that being thought of only as physically pretty may lead down a lonely or troublesome path.

If you have Pretty-Girl Syndrome or know someone who does, know that compliments are nice and appreciated, but that you are more than just physical looks. Remember that the *total package* of you is what's important in life—and that is your Body, your Brain, and your Spirit. Receiving compliments can be tricky business and a double-edged sword. Thank people for the compliments they give you, but don't put emphasis solely on compliments of the physical. Recognize your smart brain and strong spirit too. More on this later in the book.

When the Total Package Girl shows up, people find it refreshing. She is comfortable being herself, and she draws people into her circle like a magnet by being kind, happy, positive, fun, and more. Everyone seems to be attracted to the Total Package Girl. Everyone, that is, but the mean girl, who oozes envy.

. . . .

#TotalPackageGirl (n.)

A girl who is authentic (real), positive, loving, special, kind, and confident in what she does and who she is. Her total package is: her Body, her Brain, **and** her Spirit.

The **Total Package Girl** *has it all going on in one complete package; she's "all that."*

. . . .

Why doesn't the mean girl like the Total Package Girl? Because there is no stopping the Total Package Girl. Why is she unstoppable? The Total Package Girl won't play nasty games. She is too strong, too confident, too secure within herself to let a mean girl in. She is unstoppable by staying true to herself. Whether someone is wearing the trendiest clothes or a circa-2002 pair of jeans, the Total Package Girl likes the true package of each person. She is who she says she is, and she's not afraid to be herself. She just *is* the Total Package.

The **TOTAL** Package of You:

BODY

BRAIN

SPIRIT

TOTAL PACKAGE GIRL ACTIVITY:
Who Influences Me?

Have I ever done something so I could fit in, rather than doing what I deep-down really wanted to do?

☒ Yes ☐ No

What was it? Who influenced me to do it?

Wear what I wanted to wear, a friend.

Are there negative influencers who I should begin to step away from because they are not healthy for me?

NO

Have I ever avoided doing something negative even though someone tried to influence me? What was it and how did I stay strong?

Yes, I can't remember but I know it wasn't right.

What positive influencers do I have in my life?

⭐ *family* ⭐ *school*
⭐ *friends* ⭐

Real (adj.)

Actual, authentic, true, genuine; not fake.

*The Total Package Girl is **real** with herself and others; she is comfortable and centered in her Body, her Brain, and her Spirit.*

Total Package Girl Research Revealed

In a Total Package Girl survey of four hundred girls ages ten to seventeen, when asked, "Describe the Total Package Girl," girls gave the following answers:

 Confident

 Great personality and looks in one (package)

 Happy and smiles a lot

 Nice (to everyone, not mean ever), fun to be around

 Low drama, stands up for others

 Smart

 Trustworthy

 Physically attractive, pretty in her own way

 Takes care of her body

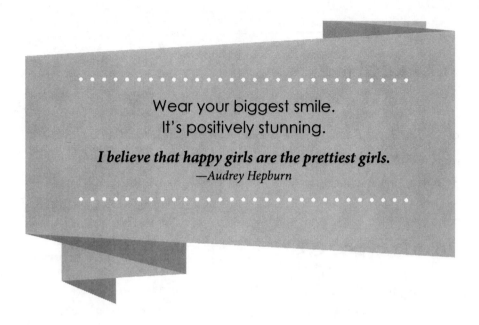

Wear your biggest smile.
It's positively stunning.

I believe that happy girls are the prettiest girls.
—Audrey Hepburn

A-ha Moment

In Total Package Global surveys, an overwhelming number of girls say they wished they were more like the Total Package Girl. Ironically, after self-analysis exercises (like the ones coming up in Part II and Part III of this book), the same girls realized that they already possessed the Total Package Girl attributes they'd listed but never knew it. They just needed to be made aware of their awesomeness!

Shine (v.)

To glow, sparkle, excel, be brilliant.

*Let the real total package of you **shine** and be celebrated by the world. Be excited and happy to #jbu.*

Your New You

#RightNow, you are joining Total Package Girls everywhere who are living the Total Package Girl life by believing in themselves, gaining confidence, and letting their own Total Package Girl attributes shine. From this moment on, realize that you are *all that*, and you can achieve your own dreams. Never be afraid to be you. Let the real inside-and-out beautiful Total Package Girl shine. Act true to your feelings and believe in yourself.

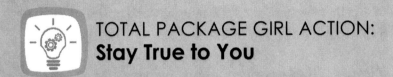

TOTAL PACKAGE GIRL ACTION:
Stay True to You

Stay true to what you believe in and do not feel the need to change and be like anyone else to fit in. What you say adds brilliance and a unique angle to every conversation—something others may never have thought about. How special is that!

Never ever be afraid to **#jbu**. When you are near a mean girl, be true to the amazing, unstoppable girl you are, inside and out, by expressing your own feelings and words. Let the mean girls play their own games and lose. Start running your own race and win. **#RightNow**

Total Package Girl Theories

Why do many girls think they aren't the Total Package Girl? Here are some theories:

> *Theory #1:* **They are uncomfortable with someone giving them props or labels, and/or putting them in a leader role.**

Terms like "the leader," "the good one," "the amazing girl" can be intimidating or make girls feel inadequate, like they can never be good enough to be called the Total Package Girl. They may feel pressure to be, look, or act a certain way. They may feel that it's easier or more comfortable to be in the role of sitting back while others lead. They need to realize that **#jbu** allows them to use their skills naturally and positions them for a role that allows them to lead and help others.

> *Theory #2:* **They have a poor body image.**

Society often dictates that girls should feel bad about their bodies if they don't look a certain way. Shouldn't every girl hate her hair, her thighs, her body type? Isn't every girl supposed to make negative comments about her body and her looks? Aren't girls supposed to wish they looked like a supermodel and if they don't, they are not so great? (This "never good enough" mentality needs to be erased. **#RightNow**)

Theory #3: **They need permission and approval.**

Some girls feel they need permission to be *all that*—that without outside approval, they aren't awesome. They may feel they aren't capable of rocking their fabulous attributes.

Theory #4: **They don't know themselves.**

When girls don't know who they are or what they stand for, they may meet "identity thieves" who contribute to them having Trying-Too-Hard Syndrome and forgetting to **#jbu**. It may then take longer for them to realize their own true attributes, values, or beliefs.

Theory #5: **They are unaware of their potential.**

Girls may never have been armed with or taught the secret weapons and tools they need to actually *be* the Total Package Girl—strong and confident in Body, Brain, and Spirit. They don't know how to lead or how to gain confidence, self-esteem, or self-worth. (Maybe that's why you are reading this book!)

Theory #6: **They haven't planted their confidence seed yet.**

Some girls don't yet realize that confidence comes from within and that who they are is good enough—in fact, it's *great* enough! Perhaps no one ever told them that it's awesome to be who they are. Once that seed is planted and begins to grow, leadership shows up, body image increases, and confidence skyrockets. (Hint: The confidence seed is planted within you now so let it grow **#RightNow!**)

Be (v.)

To live, exist, endure.

Be the Total Package Girl in your actions and your words, and you will feel powerful beyond measure. #jbu

Gain Total Package Girl Energy

It's time to:

- ✓ *Know the positive you and #jbu. Ignore identity thieves and negative influences.*

- ✓ *Eliminate the "shoulds" and the need for permission to be amazing and just go for it.*

- ✓ *Embrace and love your inner girl power and strength, and use your Total Package Girl Secret Weapons (see Part II).*

- ✓ *Know that you are amazing, and never be afraid to be all that.*

- ✓ *Eliminate the "I wish I were" mentality. The grass is never greener on the other side. Celebrate you just as you are.*

#RightNow, don't be afraid to be your amazing self. Get comfortable with being you and feel your energy increase. Test out the idea of using your powerful voice to speak up. You are as important and amazing as anyone else, so welcome to your new **#TotalPackageGirlLife!** Guess what? You are all that! Realize it; you have permission. Let it shine and reveal *you* to the world.

TOTAL PACKAGE GIRL ACTION:
Show, Don't Tell

Being the Total Package Girl doesn't mean bragging because you are so awesome (even though you are). It means showing your amazing gifts to the world through your actions. They will speak for themselves when you consistently live the **#TotalPackageGirlLife**—no bragging necessary ... **#jbu.**

Watch how awesomeness comes back to you through amazing encounters, new people you meet, and fun experiences that start showing up in your world.

Release (v.)

To set free, unleash.

Release your true inner Total Package Girl and feel your spirit soar; let you show in the actions you take and in the words you speak.

Positive energy leads
to amazing experiences. Positivity rocks!
#BeTheTotalPackageGirl

Rock (v.)

To use your power to do what you do in a fun, marvelous, and obvious way.

Rock your best self and see how much fun you have and how many amazing people come into your world! You are marvelous. You and your power rock!

Rock It, Total Package Girl!

Like Dorothy in *The Wizard of Oz*, you have the power. Although she didn't know it, Dorothy could've gotten back to Kansas because she had the power all along. All she had to do was click those heels, but she was so busy focusing on the noise surrounding her that she forgot to look at the power she'd had with her the whole time—those ruby slippers were on her feet the entire time in the Land of Oz.

You, too, have powers within you that you don't even know you have. While a nice pair of designer shoes might make you feel powerful in the short-term, it's actually your voice and your actions that express your true inner power, like those ruby slippers you've had on all along. They can take you places you never thought you could go, so don't get the Dorothy syndrome by being oblivious to your own power. Know and **#RockYourPower**.

Don't wait to be awesome.
#RockYourPower

TOTAL PACKAGE GIRL ACTIVITY:
What Power Do I Already Have?

Dorothy never knew she had the power until the very end of her adventure. #RightNow, use Dorothy's story and relate it to your life.

What power do I have at this moment that I rarely think about or give myself credit for having? Think hard.

1 _____

2 _____

3 _____

4 _____

5 _____

⭐ **My thoughts on how to use my power:**

_____

_____

_____

_____

Know Your True North

Imagine your own GPS that *you* get to set, pointed toward your own positive life dreams. How cool is that? You truly have the power (and the permission) to do that!

In your younger years—say, before the age of ten—your parents, grandparents, or teachers set your GPS for you. But as you got older, you accepted more responsibility for making smart Total Package Girl choices for yourself. Remember, with that freedom and power comes responsibility. In your **#TotalPackageGirlLife**, there will be many different roads to turn down, tough decisions to make. They're all there, sitting right in front of you. Scary and exciting, right?

R U Ready to Set Your GPS?

Fortunately, you can use your savvy Total Package Girl skills and knowledge to keep your GPS pointed in the right direction. GPS-setting is trickier the older you get, and the consequences of making poor choices are more serious. The majority of choices—the friends you make, your social media posts, your academic status and excellence—are up to you. Parents can no longer help you with homework, make decisions for you at school, or tell you what to do while you are out on a Saturday night. It's on you.

Discover (v.)

To find, bring to light, uncover.

Discover who you are and where you are going, then set your GPS on what you love doing. Self-discovery leads to amazing things.

Set your GPS to "amazing."
#TotalPackageGirl

TOTAL PACKAGE GIRL ACTIVITY:
My Amazing GPS

Who has helped me make solid decisions in my life so far?

[☒] Parents [☒] Sibling [ ] Teacher [ ] Grandparents

[ ] Other: _____

Am I ready to accept the challenge of setting my own GPS?

[☒] Yes [ ] No

Set my #TotalPackageGirlLife GPS now.
What is my destination? Why? How will I get there?

[ ] College [ ] Grad school [ ] Businesswoman

[ ] Family [ ] Superstar [ ] Scientist [ ] Musician

[ ] Professor [ ] Mom [ ] Artist [☒] Athlete

[ ] Other: _____

⭐ **My thoughts:**

work hard

Imagine this scenario: Members of a girls high school soccer team convince their coach to attend a private party with them, all in good fun. The coach, after all, wants to be the "cool" coach. At that party, the coach makes the decision to drink alcohol. Someone on the team takes a photo of her in action, although she didn't know it.

Guess where that photo of the coach drinking ended up? All over social media. Imagine her surprise and embarrassment. There were even several "favorites" and re-tweets. And guess when that coach's job ended? Right then. She was fired. The coach set her own GPS in the wrong direction, and she paid the price with the loss of her coaching job.

Ironically, the person who posted the photo at the party wasn't damaged at all and went on with her life. However, none of the soccer team members were laughing when their cool coach got fired. The coach made a poor choice based on peer pressure, to be cool, to be liked, to fit in.

She taught the team a lesson all right.

Questions: How would you feel if you were the person who posted the picture that ultimately got the coach fired? What lessons can you learn from the coach? Could the coach have been the "cool" coach by *not* going to the party at all?

TOTAL PACKAGE GIRL ACTION:
Be the #SmartChick

Every day when you get up in the morning, you get to set your GPS. Use your power: be a **#SmartChick** and set it in the right direction, doing your very best to ignore peer pressure and negative challenges that may influence you, just like they influenced the soccer coach.

Understand that there will be consequences when you make a poor decision, so at the exact moment you are faced with a tricky decision (like the moment the coach was asked to go to the party), choose *right*, not necessarily *easy* or *popular*.

When the choices you make are positive, you open up many opportunities for yourself. Stay strong when people try to tempt you and risky situations arise. Ask yourself: "Will I be happy tomorrow that I made this choice?" or "Would my grandmother be proud of my choice?" If the answer is yes, you are doing the right thing. Although it's not always easy, consistently positive choices lead to great things.

CAUTIONARY NOTE!

Every time you post a picture on Instagram—or any app of your choice—you create a digital footprint of yourself, a record of who you are choosing to be to the public. Remember this as you post. Be the #SmartChick.

Now, here's a related soccer team scenario: Imagine a soccer player on the same team who wasn't invited to that party where the coach was drinking. Rather than feel sorry for herself that she was excluded, she chose to go to the gym to work on her strength and speed.

After her workout, she went home and studied for an upcoming test. She made the most of her night while others were at the party. She refocused her negative energy on positive actions. The following Monday, she aced her test, and she went to the gym to continue her positive habit of working out to get faster and stronger … a win/win for her in the end.

Smart GPS-Setting

As you set your GPS to your true north, line it up with:

 Who you are and where you want to go in life

 What you believe, not what you think others want you to believe

 People whose values and decision-making align with yours

 What you are good at (talents) and what you enjoy doing (loves)

 What and who makes you happy (positive people and energy)

 Opportunities for growth and improvement

 Right, not wrong

 Emphasis on a healthy Body, Brain, and Spirit #TotalPackageLifestyle

 Having healthy fun and achieving your dreams

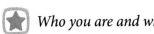 *Doing good for others; sheer kindness*

#RightNow it's time to
seal the deal and make a
Total Package Girl pact
with yourself >>>

Total Package Girl Pact

#RightNow, I begin my Total Package Girl journey, a life of trusting and continuing to build my inner power and skills to impact my world in a positive way.

I will love, respect, and trust myself and will honor the Total Package Girl philosophy. I will be positive, and I vow to make smart, healthy choices every day of my life. I will choose loving relationships with parents, friends, and family, and I will reach out to those in need with love and kindness. Every day, I will commit to taking care of my Body, sharpening my Brain, and being strong in Spirit. I will let my true Total Package Girl shine.

To the best of my ability, from this day on, I will be 100 percent committed to the Total Package Lifestyle and to myself, focusing on positive dreams and goals and keeping them front and center for life.

Each step I take on my Total Package Girl path will be more positive, powerful, loving, and amazing than the last.

Signed:

Date:

Notes:

PART II

Five Secret Weapons
of the
Total Package Girl

Total Package Girl Secret Weapons Revealed

Your secret weapons keep you savvy and smart. They are tools and skills that help you get through exciting experiences, peer-pressure moments, and relationship challenges. Whatever the situation, secret weapons have your back.

Some secret weapons you already have within you. You simply need to learn how to dig deep inside and use them. Get ready to learn five of the top secret weapons of the Total Package Girl. They will stay with you like a BFF.

. . . .

Secret Weapons (n.)

The inside knowledge, tools, and skills that Total Package Girls own; used as guides for a positive path through life.

Total Package Girls have **secret weapons** *that help them stay confident and strong.*

. . . .

Be Your Own Detective

There are times when you must find your own answers, get the facts straight, and help yourself ... be the detective in your life. These are the times when no one is going to tell you how to do things; times when you must figure things out by yourself. This might mean detecting who the mean girls are, who does drugs, or who cheats. Being the detective means you gather your own information and use it to make smarter decisions and discover the **#SmartChick** thing to do.

Imagine this scenario: Someone you don't know very well invites you to a weekend party on a Saturday night and says the party will be alcohol-free—but you're pretty sure this person has been a frequent partygoer in the past, and that those parties have involved alcohol.

You need to be your own detective and research the whole situation ahead of time. If you don't, you may get yourself in trouble by arriving at the party only to find that everyone is underage-drinking, including the person who invited you to the party ... awkward, not to mention unsafe. So be your own detective and check it out ahead of time.

Ever hear a gossipy story or a mean comment and believe it? Like if someone tells you the exam is comprehensive and you need to know everything from the entire year for it. You start worrying obsessively, studying everything you can, spending hours doing so, only to realize that the person who told you was making up a story to play a trick on you, and the exam wasn't even hard.

If you had done your detective work, you'd have realized it was a ridiculous joke from an unreliable source. You forgot to consider the source and probably should have just asked the class instructor. Sharpen those detective skills and check your facts.

TOTAL PACKAGE GIRL ACTION:
Fact Check

With Secret Weapon #1, you are the detective, meaning it's up to you to get the back story on people and situations. Take responsibility and know what you are getting into ahead of time, who you are hanging out with, and what their pattern of behavior is. Pretend you are the sweeper in the sport of curling—going ahead of the stone and guiding it on its path for a successful run.

Get the facts ahead of time, be wise, and protect yourself. And don't believe every gossipy story you hear.

Know the Difference Between What Matters and What Doesn't

Sometimes in life, it may seem like everything is a big deal, but it truly may not be. With Total Package Girl Secret Weapon #1, being your own detective means knowing that some things in life just don't matter as much as you think they do. So before you get overly dramatic or worried about something, ask yourself, "Does this really matter in the big picture of my life?"

On the flip side, some things really do matter in life even though they aren't screaming at you to pay attention to them. They may be very quiet but need your attention—like a sick grandparent who has a quiet yet chronic cough, or an exam that is steadily creeping up on you. Be a detective and uncover the difference between things that truly matter and things you can dismiss altogether and ignore.

In your world, you already know that there can be a lot of noise. Sometimes it's for reasons that don't matter at all, such as when a dramatic student in class loudly and frequently complains that she or he isn't called on enough. This really doesn't matter at all, yet it may be very noisy and distracting.

Push things that don't matter away from your brain and try to filter them out. This will help you focus on what truly does matter. Prioritizing life's big things will help you realize how little the little things matter.

If you drop your book in the hallway in front of lots of people and it makes a loud noise and everybody looks, that's a little thing and it doesn't matter. Everybody drops a book or something at some point. Who really cares how many people are watching? Laugh it off, push it out of your mind. Doesn't matter a bit. Conversely, if you learn that your cousin has developed a serious illness, that's a big thing, and it matters a lot. Spend your time caring for your cousin and not the class drama queen or king or the seemingly embarrassing book drop.

Use the Total Package Girl Noise Spectrum tool on the next page to identify what truly matters and what doesn't. Simply plot items from your life on the grid to see if they truly matter or are merely unimportant noise. This Total Package Girl tool will help you be your own detective and get rid of noisy people or drama that doesn't matter in life.

A comment that someone makes about your looks, clothes, a spilled glass of water, or a silly mistake you've made completely doesn't matter and goes in the lower right quadrant: *Noisy/Doesn't Matter*. Spend little or no energy or time on people or comments in that quadrant. On the other hand, noise from a child screaming because she broke her arm, goes in the top right quadrant: *Noisy/Matters*. That child needs medical attention.

Once you plot life noise on the Noise Spectrum, it's easier to laugh things off that are silly or ridiculous. Definitely pay attention to and spend time on the important things, like the health of your grandmother, a sick pet, school projects, those who need assistance, and things that truly make a difference in life. They may be quiet, but they really matter. That's where your time is spent wisely.

Focus your energy on the top half of the Total Package Girl Noise Spectrum. Those things matter. The bottom half is insignificant noise.

TOTAL PACKAGE GIRL TOOL:
Noise Spectrum
What Matters and What's Just Noise?

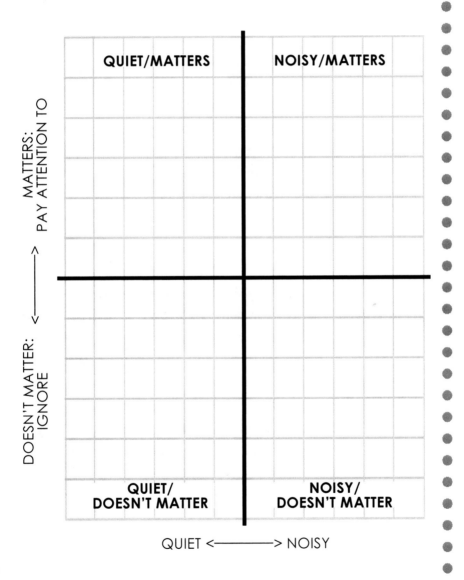

Know Your Reactions

Pay attention to how you react to things. Does it matter if you're being laughed at or made fun of for something silly? Probably not, but your reaction matters.

If people are immature and laugh at you repeatedly, they are most likely looking for a reaction from you (sounds ridiculous, but people really do that). Try not to provide a reaction, such as showing embarrassment, talking back, or doing to them what they did to you. For example, if you give certain mean girls the embarrassed reaction they are looking for, chances are they will repeat their behavior. Do your best to respond in an assertive way, without reacting negatively.

CAUTIONARY NOTE!

If others' negative actions become harassing, humiliating, and/or occur with regularity, it's time to take a different approach and talk with a trusted adult immediately to get reinforcement, and then get help from a professional (such as a psychologist, guidance counselor, clergy, or physician) as needed. Enough is enough.

Know When It's Time to Move On

Sometimes you need to move on from a situation, such as when:

❋ *People don't have your back.*

❋ *People consistently make fun of you.*

❋ *The situation is unhealthy or not fun anymore.*

❋ *You're on a different path than your dreams and goals.*

Let the Noise Spectrum help guide you in your decision.

 TOTAL PACKAGE GIRL ACTIVITY:
Detect Things That Do and Don't Matter in My Life

What noisy people or things in my life have I been spending too much time on that don't matter? (*Use the Noise Spectrum.*)

☒ Dramatic people   ☐ Certain activities

☐ Mean people   ☒ Online/social media activities

☐ Other: _____

What things in my life are quiet but need attention?

☐ Sick relative or friend   ☐ Person being bullied

☒ Upcoming exam   ☒ Other: Family

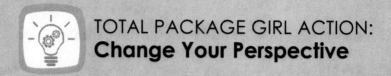

TOTAL PACKAGE GIRL ACTION:
Change Your Perspective

When something is bothersome, do this exercise to look at it more clearly: Picture yourself on a mountaintop 10,000 feet in the sky looking down on one side of the mountain and listening in on the girls below who are all super-worried about what they look like, moving in circles like ants, fretting about what they will wear, whispering about one another, and laughing at each others' clothing. They scurry about worrying about what piece of cloth another human is wearing.

You then look to the other side of the mountain and see people who are cold and huddled together, who have very little to wear, who are trying to find food to eat, searching in the fields, crying because they don't know if their children will have food to survive another day.

Now, which scenario really matters and needs attention? Which doesn't? It's a matter of perspective and pretty easy to see when you're up above the situation, don't you agree? Remember this mountaintop view when you get in your own situations, and if something is truly unimportant, move on. Total Package Girls are detectives and understand that spending time on relevant things in life is where it's at.

Dig Deeper: Things Aren't Always as They Seem

Imagine this scenario: At the mall, you find the exact new phone you've been wanting, and it's on sale for half price. But then you see that the price doesn't include service charges, hook-up, monthly fees, accessories, etc. Ugh! When things are too perfect to be true on the surface, they probably are.

When something sounds too good to be true, when things just don't look right, when someone appears not to be telling the whole truth, dig deeper.

Insight: If you see a commercial where a famous fifty-year-old woman is selling her makeup line and you hear her friends use terms like, "She looks like she's twenty" or "She's showing up her teenage daughter," dig deeper and realize a few things:

❊ *She's there to sell makeup to make money.*

❊ *The writer of the TV commercial used the "me too" sales technique, because everyone wants to look like a famous woman who looks like a teenager, right?*

❊ *Camera lenses, camera angles, and lighting can do amazing things.*

❊ *Airbrushing and certain computer techniques can eliminate wrinkles, alter body size and shape, and change facial features.*

SECRET WEAPON #1

❋ *The product line advertised doesn't include other techniques that may have been used by that famous woman, such as facial fillers or injections.*

Let's be honest: no fifty-year-old woman looks like she's twenty. Be the detective and ask yourself what doesn't look right. What's really going on? You've probably seen videos that reveal how models are altered and "transformed" through deceptive techniques. You know the ones, where everyday girls and women are elongated and airbrushed. It happens regularly so don't be fooled. Dig deeper for the truth when things just don't look right.

If you could float around with your invisibility cloak like in J. K. Rowling's *Harry Potter and the Sorcerer's Stone*, you'd see that the back story on many things is not what it appears to be. You'd see that people you thought were perfect, such as television or movie actresses and models, are imperfectly human. They have acne, cellulite, wrinkles, struggling relationships, and they make mistakes ... just like everyone else on this earth. That cloak would change your view forever of what happens behind the scenes.

Not only are you a detective, but you're also smart enough to realize that things aren't always as they seem, and you no longer have to believe—or act on—the hype. Be savvy and dig deeper. Sometimes, things that just don't look right, aren't.

 Know That Your Mind Can Make Things Up

Ever felt like everyone is staring at you, secretly making fun of your clothes or your hair? Truth is, you may very well be making that scenario up in your mind because you don't like your hair or your clothes that day. Because you don't feel confident, you think everyone is staring. You make up a scenario that feeds upon your insecurities.

If you're embarrassed or think you look stupid because you have acne ... guess what? Many other teenagers have pimples on occasion too. While you're busy worrying about yours, they're busy worrying about theirs! You think you're having a bad hair day? Well, your hair might be the envy of other girls who believe *they* are having a bad hair day, and you don't even know it. So stop making up insecurities in your head. Catch yourself doing so, and laugh at these made-up thoughts. Resolve to **#jbu** and use that energy to have more fun! When your brain plays games with you based on an unnecessary worry or insecurity, push those head games aside and call out your brain!

TOTAL PACKAGE GIRL ACTIVITY:
What Are My Made-Up Thoughts?

What do I feel insecure about because something isn't perfectly perfect?

☒ Body   ☐ Hair   ☒ Face

☐ Other: _____

What steps can I take to feel more secure about them?

① work out   ② not care

③ love myself   ④ just live life

That Girl: A Story

Remember when That Girl felt self-conscious and insecure because she wore hand-me-down clothes and she felt that everyone else had such pretty new clothes? What she didn't know then was:

* ❄ No one even knew she was wearing hand-me-downs.

* ❄ Others really liked what she was wearing even though they didn't tell her.

* ❄ Many other girls in her grade also were wearing hand-me-downs and felt self-conscious at the same time she did.

That Girl created an insecurity that wasn't there. If she'd called out her brain, her insecurity would have vanished, clearing the way for happier, more confident times and less worry about her looks or being good enough.

As she got older, That Girl began to get more comfortable with herself, her clothes, her likes, and her dislikes. The hand-me-downs began to not matter. She grew to like her look in the mirror—even that scar on her forehead was part of who she was—and when she got contacts, she felt like she no longer had to hide behind the thick glasses. This really helped her timidness.

She started to find her confidence in activities she loved and was good at. She met a couple of really amazing and true friends. She was exploring more new friendships, finding her talents, and doing what she loved to do. But she still worried.

 Stop Worrying and *Act*

It's okay *not* to worry, girls—even though sometimes you may think you're supposed to worry. You see your mom, dad, or your grandparents worrying, so you get in the habit of doing the same. If you are a worrier like *That Girl*, begin to notice when you worry and stop yourself.

There are some things you can't control, like the weather or what someone else says, or what happens on the other side of the world. So if you find yourself worrying a lot about these things, one way to deal with it is to take action and do something about it. Act in direct response to whatever it is you are worried about, because truly, worrying can make things worse. When you worry or have thoughts about things that are completely out of your control, you increase your stress dramatically, zapping the fun right out of life, or putting you at risk of getting sick. This isn't like a Total Package Girl at all! You *want* fun in your life!

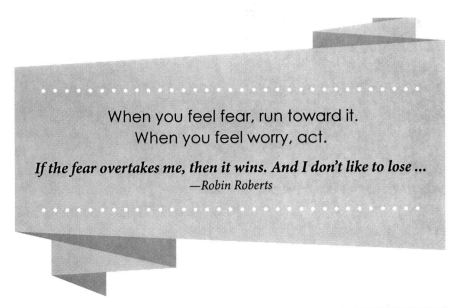

When you feel fear, run toward it.
When you feel worry, act.

If the fear overtakes me, then it wins. And I don't like to lose ...
—*Robin Roberts*

TOTAL PACKAGE GIRL ACTION:
Less Worry, More Confidence

Maybe you're worried about getting poor grades in school or not performing well in the upcoming game. Maybe you're afraid that a certain group of kids won't accept you. Maybe you're worried that you won't get a good score on the ACT or SAT exam. Maybe it's a homecoming school dance or event that's worrying you. This is called what-if thinking—worrying about things that haven't even happened yet.

Let's say your bus is late and you start worrying, "What if I am late to school? What if I get a tardy slip?" *Act* by halting worry in its tracks and tell your brain, "Stop!" Then use logic and play out the situation. Tell yourself that the timing of the bus is completely out of your control. Tell yourself you will relax and handle whatever the result of the bus being late is. Laugh and call your worry "silly." Allow yourself to relax, take a breath, and realize that the school principal will know that your bus is running behind schedule and you will not get a tardy slip. You are not going to be in trouble at all.

If you're worried about grades, *act* by getting the study guide for your ACT or SAT exam. *Act* by preparing well for the exam. If you're worried about performing well at your sport, *act* by going to a trainer before the season starts. *Act* by practicing the technical aspects of your sport ahead of time to alleviate or minimize worry.

A little self-talk and a lot of action make all the difference when it comes to letting go of worry. When you *act*, you feel better-prepared and more confident, like you're doing something about the thing you are worried about. Action can take the worry right out of a situation.

So, **#RightNow**, begin to train yourself *not* to worry. Catch yourself, and when you start feeling a worry coming on, tell yourself it's going to be okay. Just like you did with the bus, use logic and then trust yourself to deal with the consequences as they unfold—if there *are* any consequences. (Your mind might have made those up!)

What-if thinking means you are imagining a scenario that may never ever happen. Get comfortable with *not* knowing everything in advance. Take life's events as they come at you and begin to let go of worry like you'd release a helium balloon into the sky. Train your brain to go with the flow. Once you get the hang of not worrying, it's super-refreshing, and life is much more fun.

CAUTIONARY NOTE!

It's okay to ask for help, particularly if your worrying ever gets out of control and you feel super-scared often. Talk to your parents or school counselor. Never be embarrassed to ask for help. It's brave!

Know When You Know

Ever ask your parents if it's okay to go to an eleven p.m. movie on a weeknight? You know when you know, and you already know that answer!

Many times, you already know the right answer and what to do. Your intuition tells you. Yet you may be in the habit of always asking someone else for an opinion, or wanting someone else to tell you you're right, or getting approval to do something you already know is okay. At those times, try to quiet your mind and hear the answer loud and clear coming from your inner girl, and trust what you know to be true. You don't always need to ask for help. Sometimes the answer lies within you. You just need to detect it on your own.

Rethink Drama

Sometimes people with a lot of drama in their lives may actually be lonely. Once you detect this, you can become more caring about them, which can take a lot of pressure off of uncomfortable or dramatic situations. True, that?

We've all met people who repeatedly make up grand stories, exaggerate, or publicly act in outrageous or dramatic ways, perhaps for attention. Consider that it's likely they feel they aren't getting enough love and attention so they do this to get some. They may feel lonely inside for reasons you don't understand. Perhaps they lost their mother at an early age, or perhaps their father is in jail, and they are really sad, lonely, or embarrassed on the inside. They are trying hard to get others to look at them and pay attention to them perhaps through gossip, dramatic stories, or publicly crying about something that seems trivial to you. The point is, *you just don't know what is really going on inside a person.* Be sensitive, keep your eyes open, and if you see dramatic situations like these, look at the person creating the drama and understand that something else may possibly be going on. Particularly if this is a pattern, this person may need help, or a hug, or simply to hear you say, "I understand."

If you're the one who's often dramatic, talk to an adult, get some hugs from your grandparents or your little sibling, or spend time with a pet. These things can add love to life and make you feel special again, like you truly are! Seek professional help if needed.

 Follow Your Own GPS

 You already know you get to set your own GPS much of the time. When set in a positive direction, it's a great guide to your dreams. When set in the wrong direction, it can lead to all kinds of trouble. For example, a GPS can point you toward bodily injury or health issues when set on, say, risky behavior like drinking alcohol or doing drugs. Set your GPS on smart actions that lead you away from trouble and toward awesome people and amazing dreams.

Be the detective and use your GPS to detect when someone tries to tempt you into doing something you aren't comfortable with or that you know is wrong or illegal, like experimenting with drugs. At that **#RightNow** moment, think about things like these:

* ✣ *How will this action affect my amazing dreams?*

* ✣ *What are the consequences of getting caught by my parents, the school principal, my teachers?*

* ✣ *What effect will this have on my body or my health?*

* ✣ *What professional, public, or social ramifications will there be—for example, if others take pictures of me acting illegally and post them on Instagram, might that keep me from getting a job in the future?*

People will try to pressure you in life. They likely don't have the solid GPS that you do. In fact, they may have no GPS at all, and may be on a downward spiral to nowhere, hoping to pull you down too. Follow your GPS.

 ## Rehearse for Future Tricky Times

Challenges are a part of life. They will happen, so being ready for them pays off when tricky situations actually occur. Preparation makes you more confident, like being in the school play and rehearsing your lines over and over again. You then know your lines so well ahead of time that you can confidently walk out on that stage at the performance and blow the socks off the audience.

Rehearsal is one of the best ways to prepare yourself for real-life scenarios as well. Mentally or physically playing out life's tricky situations will help tremendously. Imagine challenging or scary situations that could come your way: confrontation with a mean person in a school hallway, watching a friend being bullied, dealing with an impatient teacher, someone asking you on a date.

What other situations might you come across that could be scary, awkward, or tough?

Mentally play out those scenarios and then discuss them with a friend or parent before they ever happen. Get comfortable with how you would respond, and where you stand when faced head-on with uncomfortable, confusing, or conflict-oriented situations. This preparation will help you so much when you are actually *in* an uncomfortable, tricky encounter. Preparation builds confidence.

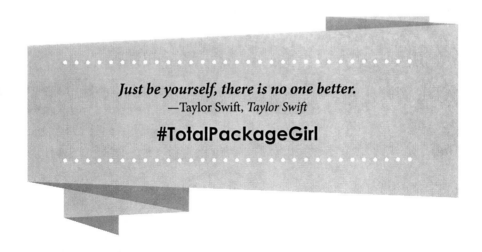

Just be yourself, there is no one better.
—Taylor Swift, *Taylor Swift*
#TotalPackageGirl

That Girl: A Story

When young, That Girl and her best friend used to play in their front yards every single day of summer. Cars would drive by and they'd play the game of waving to see if that driver would wave back. One day when they waved to a strange old car, it pulled over and rolled down the window, asking them to come over and pet a puppy.

That Girl's mother had always taught her (and made her role play) stranger danger, having her yell "No!" and run back into the house if an unknown car stopped and the people inside called her to "come here."

She and her friend had practiced that scenario before, but they'd never experienced the real-life situation. In that moment, That Girl and her best friend could have frozen in fear, but they didn't. In fact, they knew exactly what to do. In a split second, they screamed "No!" in unison and sprinted as fast as they could back into the house and told That Girl's mother what had happened.

Their preparation—the rehearsal—had paid off big-time when they knew exactly what to do in that high-risk situation as soon as the stranger's car pulled up to them. They were safe because they knew how to do the right thing in that moment. They later learned that the car was involved in an attempted kidnapping in the area.

The lesson *That Girl* and her best friend learned as kids applies to teenagers as well. Regarding issues like smoking or posting negative photos on social media, know how to say "No!" just like the two girls did as kids. It paid for them to be prepared as kids, and now it pays because that exact lesson can be used later in life. Now, if they are ever asked to drink alcohol or smoke marijuana, *That Girl* and her best friend can vividly remember like it was yesterday the yelling of "No!" when they were kids, and they know to walk away just as they did then.

Preparation and rehearsing experiences early in life helps you stay away from peer pressure and negative influencers later in life.

Total Package Girl Rehearsal and Preparation Tactics

 Talk to the mirror.

 Use your cell phone or your laptop to record yourself playing out a possible scenario and what you'd say or do.

 Role play with an adult or friend and discuss any or every imagined scenario that might come up.

The more prepared you are with the details of each anticipated scenario, the more empowered and confident you'll be when handling those tricky situations.

 Stay Ahead of the Game

Ever procrastinate? You know, put some long or boring task off until the very, very, very last minute (ahem, studying for an exam)?

Procrastination is sometimes easier than facing a job that takes a lot of effort, right? Yet it can also increase stress, anxiety, and drama in your life, and can even decrease your self-esteem. Who needs that anyway?

If you find yourself being the classic procrastinator, take control by:

 Making a list of all upcoming to-dos

 Prioritizing what needs to get done first

 Breaking big tasks into small pieces

 Jumping on big projects early in the process, like right away

Doing these steps gives you more time to focus on the quality of the project so you aren't just throwing something together. Your goal is to do a quality, amazing job, not a half-hearted job.

Make it a habit to get things done ASAP. This way, they are out of your way, and that's refreshing. It also frees up time for other, more fun activities. For example, if your family is leaving for a spring-break vacation and you know you have a huge project that will be due the day you return from break, plan ahead, do the work before you leave for vacation, and get the project done early so that when you return, you don't have to stay up half the night completing it because you procrastinated.

Be your own detective, think ahead, and get the work done early. Fight the urge to procrastinate. You will be happy you did. If you want more information on how *not* to procrastinate, check out **TotalPackageGirl.com** and get the Total Package Professional time management success tool.

Make the Most of Every Life Experience

Make everything you do and every experience you encounter positive and a great life experience. You can learn a lesson from each new person who comes into your world and each new adventure you explore. Although it's hard to imagine, even a bad experience can turn out to be good if you learn from it.

The same can be true with your career. If you happen to be a doctor, be the best, most knowledgeable, most caring doctor you can be. Enjoy meeting your patients, treat them with respect, and have fun talking with them and hearing about their life experiences. Research your field, study, and know the latest technologies.

If you are on a vacation and decide to go parasailing for the first time, enjoy getting in the boat, strapping on the safety harness, and lifting slowly up into the sky. Enjoy the view while you are soaring above the sea. Take it all in, enjoy the little details, and max out your experience. Be positive and pull out the fun, the learning, the feeling you get.

Making the most of every life situation might mean looking at something completely differently than you ever have; changing things up a bit; being curious and asking lots of questions; or trying something new. This is a beautiful gift of the Total Package Girl—to *positively* max out your experiences and teach others to do the same. Be in the **#RightNow** moment.

That Girl: A Story

That Girl is now the pitcher on the mound in the championship game, bottom of the ninth with one out. She pitches it over the plate; the batter smacks a pop fly into deep foul territory. She feels her legs running like the wind toward first base to get to the ball, the fastest she's ever run, fearlessly diving and ultimately catching the nearly impossible pop fly in foul territory to make it two outs in the bottom of the ninth.

The fans go crazy, thinking there was no chance she'd catch that ball. But she did, with a boatload of effort and determination. Now, two outs. She faces the top of the batting order to end the inning and win the game. One of the opponent's best hitters is up to bat. That Girl battles foul ball after foul ball, then she pitches three straight balls. Now it's a 3-2 count. Next pitch, this batter smacks a line drive down low to That Girl's left. She dives, opens her glove into the path of the ball, and "smack!" It finds the pocket of That Girl's glove. She rolls onto the ground and checks to make sure the ball is in her glove, and sure enough, it is! Out number three, game over.

Her team wins the championship! She's the winning pitcher. It was a team effort, and getting the last two outs was serious get-in-the-zone time for That Girl.

After many congrats from others, and after wiping the blood from her knee, That Girl pondered, "What was the secret to getting the last two outs? Luck? Skill?" Truth is, she'd helped herself out and maximized the challenging game situation. All of her hours of practicing on the field taking line drives and grounders had paid off. Her job had been to get the batters out, to end that ninth inning battle, and to win the game.

By making that extra effort, through sheer determination, focus, and bringing her "A" game, she left it all on the field, made the last two outs to get out of a pinch, out of the inning, and into the winner's circle. She and her team had worked hard all season and in the off-season. Now, she helped her team get it done and make the most of their season. She had a champion mindset. Her confidence was soaring.

. . . .

Get the Edge With a Champion Mindset

That Girl began with the end in mind. She started the game believing she was going to win ..: to play her best … to be a champion. She was driven to get the edge.

When you take a test, know that you are going to conquer that essay and get 100 percent. Know, just like *That Girl* did, that whenever you can, you are going to help yourself be better, achieve more, get the edge, and be your most awesome self.

Do your best, give your best, be your best.
#TotalPackageLifestyle

10 Ways to Be Awesome in All You Do

1 *If you love and want something, work hard for it.* Don't give up when others are discouraging, when things get tough, or when you're too tired. Tell yourself, "Five minutes more."

2 *Know how success will be measured.* Know what the boss or the coach or the teacher is looking for in order to achieve success. Know the rubric, the goal, and the expected outcome. Is it to win, to get an A, to get into the college of your choice? Then meet it and exceed it!

3 *Learn and read everything you can* to be your best academically, professionally, and socially.

4 *Get the job done early,* expect obstacles, know your timeline for completion, and meet or beat it.

5 *Push through challenging times and difficult situations.* Never give up. Instead, hunker down, dig your heels in, and stay with it. Quitting isn't an option (unless there is behavior or treatment occurring that involves health or safety issues).

6 *Don't wait for others to go first.* Be the first to step up and volunteer to do the work. Sitting back and watching others do all the work, or letting others in your group do the job for you, isn't the Total Package Girl way. Do things well, be the first to help the person being bullied, or to win the competition fair and square. Work hard. Help out. Dive in first.

7 *Seal the deal.* When given the chance, seal the deal the way *That Girl* the pitcher did. In other words, look to help clinch the outcome of a situation when the opportunity presents itself. *That Girl* left everything on the field. Even if someone looks better than you on the court or in the competition, do not get intimidated but trust in your own abilities.

8 *Go the extra mile to help, to do, to be better.* Do the unexpected. Give 110 percent. If work ends at 5 p.m., don't leave at 4:50. Stay as late as needed. Life doesn't give freebies very often, and no one is going to walk up to you and hand you a good grade, an award, a college scholarship, or a promotion unless you've worked for it. As with the pitcher, hard work and effort will pay off. Teachers, parents, and bosses reward hard work. Teachers are more likely to give you the benefit at the end of the semester if you are, say, between an "A" and a "B," if they know how hard you've worked all along.

If you deeply want and need something in life, go get it. Nothing can stand in your way if you have self-motivation and the desire to succeed.

#TotalPackageGirl

9 **Go get it.** A boy at a basketball camp was listening to a coach discuss how to be excellent at the game of basketball. The coach held up a twenty-dollar bill and asked, "How many of you here today want this?" So of course, every boy in the group raised his hand. Next the coach asked, "How many of you *really* want this?" Raised hands all around. Then he asked, "How are you going to get it?" Some boys sat quietly pondering the question. A couple responded with, "Work hard." But one boy got up, walked over to the coach, and snatched the twenty-dollar bill from the coach's hand. The coach grinned and said, "Now that's what I'm talking about. If you want something in life, you gotta go get it." The boy went home from camp twenty dollars richer.

10 *Make things fun.* Look for the happiness or fun in things. Smile. People like being around happy people. Not everything in life is in the "fun" category for sure, but you can still learn all you can or be the best you can be to make the most of a happy or a trying situation. Make it fun whenever you can!

All of these ten things can bring out your best, make your spirit soar, make others feel like a million bucks, and give you the edge in awesomeness.

Be Your Own Detective

✅ **Know the Difference Between What Matters and What Doesn't**

✅ **Know Your Reactions**

✅ **Know When It's Time to Move On**

✅ **Dig Deeper: Things Aren't Always as They Seem**

✅ **Know That Your Mind Can Make Things Up**

✅ **Stop Worrying and *Act***

✅ **Know When You Know**

✅ **Rethink Drama**

✅ **Follow Your Own GPS**

✅ **Rehearse for Future Tricky Times**

✅ **Stay Ahead of the Game**

✅ **Make the Most Out of Every Life Experience**

✅ **Get the Edge With a Champion Mindset**

Surround Yourself with TruBlues

Ever had a best buddy? If you're lucky enough to be able to say yes, then you know how good it feels to have someone you can depend on, a go-to person to talk to or hang out with. Different years may mean different friends, so you may or may not have a BFF now in your life. In the big picture of life, it is healthy and fun to feel loved, respected, and awesome to another person and to give that to them in return. At Total Package Global, a trusting, dependable person in your life is called a TruBlue.

. . . .

#TruBlue (n.)

A high-quality, trustworthy person who is loyal and steady no matter what; dependable, a personal cheerleader, and a truth-teller. Someone who stands by you, listens without judgment, provides clarity when you are confused, doesn't turn on you, and loves you for you.

*A **TruBlue** believes in you, and loves and respects the real you.*

. . . .

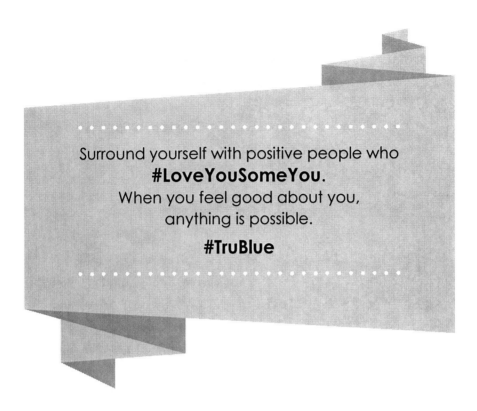

Surround yourself with positive people who
#LoveYouSomeYou.
When you feel good about you,
anything is possible.
#TruBlue

TruBlues in Action

TruBlues share your values, which may include trust, loyalty, and ambition. Sometimes TruBlues appear in less-than-obvious places. They vary in age, looks, and geographic location. A TruBlue could be a grandparent, neighbor, teacher, sibling, cousin, or long-lost friend. You could meet a TruBlue at the mall, at worship, at the gym, anywhere. A TruBlue's friendship is proven through tough times and fun times too. It is said, "To the world you are one person, to one person you may be the world."

On the opposite end of the spectrum, ever have those "friends" who can't keep a secret or who would throw you under the bus at any time? Well, no one needs that! That is no TruBlue.

It can be hard finding TruBlues, but they also can be right under your nose if you are looking. If you don't yet have a TruBlue, try looking in less obvious places. We're talking about that steady person in your life you can rely on, talk to, get hugs from, get the truth from, and get no judgment from—someone who will go the extra mile to give help or support when you feel awful, make you laugh when you're sad, or notice when you're not yourself and ask, "What's up?" TruBlues aren't perfect, but they are consistently there for you.

Sometimes the world makes it seem like you need a gazillion friends. Not so. More important than quantity is having a quality person (or two or three) who doesn't tell anyone your secrets, who loves and respects you for you, and who can help you when times get tough. TruBlues help pull you through, and you do the same for them. And, yes, TruBlues are truly happy for you when good things happen to you.

Insight: Our research shows that having a strong support network gives girls confidence, which leads to smarter decisions in a girl's life.

The Anti-TruBlue in Action

The opposite of TruBlues exists too, and you know the type—nice one day and not nice the next. Anti-TruBlues may not be as mean as a mean girl, but they may only talk to you when they need something or when you're the only one around. They may be disrespectful to you as well.

Take steps to replace an anti-TruBlue with a TruBlue when possible. When it comes to friends, the number of friends doesn't matter, but the quality of the friendship does. Stay near your TruBlues.

. . . .

Discern (v.)

To distinguish, detect; to know the difference—between right and wrong, for example—and to determine the right thing to do.

*Learn to **discern** mean girls from Total Package Girls, and TruBlues from anti-TruBlues.*

. . . .

Not Sure Who's Who?

TruBlues have your back. Anti-TruBlues do not. You'll definitely know a TruBlue because the relationship is easier and makes you feel like you can **#jbu**. You don't have to try too hard to fit in. On the flip side, you'll know anti-TruBlues because some days they are nice and other days they'll dump you for someone else. They may even bad-mouth you to others or in front of others. They won't include you in their activities (but may want to be included in yours), and they may make fun of your mistakes. Discerning the difference and feeling how much more positive you are around TruBlues makes it easier to courageously walk away from anti-TruBlues.

That Girl: A Story

That Girl kept looking for the positive throughout junior high and high school. She stayed positive and started to focus on her future and not worry about the little things she couldn't control.

One day her TruBlue teacher and role model told her she was good at something—communications—and that she would be great at public relations and broadcasting, a career she'd never thought about before that very moment. The seed of confidence began to grow. She researched the idea, thought about it, prayed about it.

That Girl chose this field as her college major because someone she trusted told her she would be good at it. That Girl's role model had exposed her to a potential talent. And she grew even more confident inside.

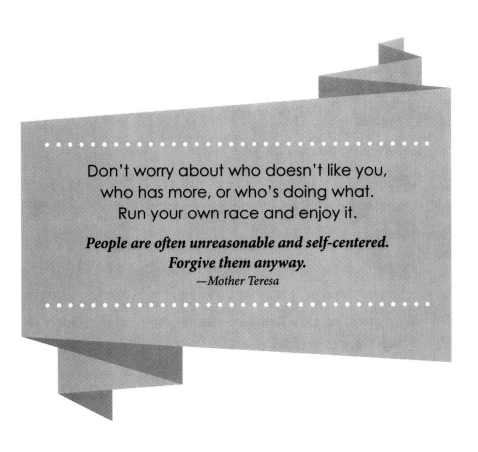

Don't worry about who doesn't like you,
who has more, or who's doing what.
Run your own race and enjoy it.

People are often unreasonable and self-centered.
Forgive them anyway.
—*Mother Teresa*

Shout-Out (n.)

Public expression of thanks or gratitude.

*I would like to give a **shout-out** to the steadfast love and support of my TruBlues, one of life's rarest blessings. **#TruBlue***

TOTAL PACKAGE GIRL ACTIVITY:
Who Are My TruBlues?

Who are my TruBlues?

⭐ _____

⭐ _____

⭐ _____

Who are some anti-TruBlues—those who treat me poorly yet I keep them in my life?

◻ _____

◻ _____

◻ _____

How can I bring and keep TruBlues in my life?

◻ Make a **#SmartChick** commitment to be with respectful, loving friends.

◻ Recognize mean girls and stay away.

◻ Be a TruBlue to someone else.

◻ Other: _____

Parents as TruBlues

All parents are different. Some seem to hover over your every move. Some avoid hands-on parenting. Some show affection and some don't. Every household is different, and it's impractical to compare what is happening in your home with what's happening in someone else's.

Family dynamics and household statuses are unique too. Your parents (or guardians) may be married, divorced, or single, or you may have a blended family. Whatever your family situation, set a goal to be on the same team as your parents. They can be your TruBlues in terms of trusting, loving, confiding in, and receiving advice from them. Do your very best and make a huge effort to get along with them.

No matter how frustrating or annoying the relationship with your parents may be at times, having mutual respect is critical. Understand that disagreements are normal in a family. Also know that it's okay to have and respectfully express your own opinions that may differ from your parents.

Parents need your respect and love, so learning to be patient is important. Most parents are doing the best they can to raise you well and keep you safe, using whatever tools they were born and raised with. They may or may not have had the best role models in their own lives, but they want to raise you in the best way possible. Most aren't looking to fill your BFF spot but can be there as people to rely on.

●　●　●　●　●　●　●　●　●　●　●　●　●　●　●　●　●　●　●　●

Note: When communicating with parents, use your voice in a productive manner, be courteous and helpful, give them hugs when they least expect them, and find ways to show love and respect.

TOTAL PACKAGE GIRL ACTIVITY:
My Family

Describe my family:

Size:

How we get along:

Other:

My relationship with my parents (guardians) is:

☐ Easy ☐ Tough ☐ Middle

The energy in my household is:

☐ Fun ☐ Stressful

☐ Happy overall ☐ Unhappy overall

☐ Normal ☐ Abnormal ☐ Other

Who do I talk to the best?

How could my household relationships be better? What is my role in this improvement?

⭐

⭐

Parents make mistakes and don't know everything, but they have gone through many teachable moments. Learn to settle down and listen to your parents. How? You can calm down a notch by taking a deep breath, stepping away, or keeping quiet for a minute longer when you feel like disagreeing or arguing with them. Listen to them and you may receive solid advice to help you in a tough life situation.

Get Savvy with Your Parents

Remember that your parents may have had the same feelings you have now when they were your age. That means they may understand you more than you think they do. Give them a chance to explain their beliefs and opinions. Their advice may save you a lot of time, difficulty, or sadness. Here are some other tips that may help your relationship with your parents:

 Hug them every day. Know that there are little things they do for you behind the scenes that you don't know about, which may include sacrificing their own priorities for your school event, your birthday party, your game. They love you and are doing their best, so show them that you appreciate and love them.

 Know their "type." Some parents are calm, and some are more quick to get emotional. Some may be quieter, others may be the raise-their-voice type. Some are busy, preoccupied, over-involved, under-involved, critical, complimentary. Knowing your parents' type can help you to better understand and get along with them.

Communicate and keep on talking. Whatever type you may characterize your parents as, keep on talking to them, even when you want to shut down and close the lines of communication. This is super important. You need each other for overall well-being, safety, happiness, and love. Also, know when it's a good time to talk with them. When they first walk in the door from a crazy day at work may not be the best time. Know what timing works well for them and also for you, so you can keep on talking.

 Remind them that you, too, are doing your best. Parents need to hear that from you.

 Say thanks for the things they do—big or small. Want a more easy-going house? Give your parents credit by showing gratitude and saying thank you for running you around, buying you new shoes or clothes, making you dinner late at night, helping you study for a test.

 Offer comfort when they are upset. They need love too. If you notice they are having a rough or sad day, sit down and talk with them, give them a hug or a kiss, and show them compassion.

 Help around the house. Do work like cleaning your room, hanging your towels, and keeping the bathroom clean. Then, add to that list—take out the garbage, load the dishwasher, do laundry, take a shower without being told. This is huge, and it'll help you in the long run with smart life skills.

Give your best effort in school and beyond. Few things bring a parent's mood down more than when a child brings home bad grades. Discipline yourself to study hard, show effort, and get and keep your grades in order. Learn how to take the initiative to talk to your teachers, too, if you aren't doing well or are unclear in a class. Solid effort pays off for everyone.

 Keep calm when you feel an argument coming on. Use "I feel" language with parents (as outlandish as you may think this sounds): "I feel you aren't listening to my side of this" or "I feel like you are being too hard on me." This takes accusation out of the equation. Other ways to calm down include taking a walk, stepping outside if you need to simmer down and get your emotions in check, and breathing deeply.

 Remember that you are all on the same team. If you're Yankees and they're Red Sox, it will always be a battle. Your household may run more smoothly if you're both Yankees or both Red Sox (at least most of the time). You don't criticize and yell at your teammates, do you? Same principle here. Be a team player. It's okay to respectfully disagree, but no one wants constant conflict.

 Cut them a break when they fall short. If they were late to pick you up, forgot to pack you a lunch, or didn't have time to get groceries that night so you didn't have your favorite snack, be understanding. Rather than get mad, tell them it's okay. Forgive them and ask for the same when the roles are reversed.

 Let them play a role in your life. You won't always agree with them, but notice and tone down drama or attitude a bit. It's good to express and share feelings, with the goal of doing so in a productive way. Let parents enjoy your favorite—or not so favorite—moments. Tell them about your school day, your evening plans, the birthday party you attended. When they come to a school play or concert, go up to them afterward and give them a hug to show your appreciation for them being there to see you in action.

 Try to understand why they get upset with you. It may be because they know you can do better, that you can make a better choice, or that you didn't put forth your top effort. Perhaps they are having a bad day and that's why they are upset; sometimes it has nothing to do with you. If you can see the back story, it sometimes helps you to be more compassionate, and it can guide you through the situation more quickly and give you greater understanding.

 Tell them the truth, always. Lies will ruin your relationship. Once you've broken the trust, it's hard to regain, so no lies.

CAUTIONARY NOTE!

Physical confrontations or violence are not okay when it comes to relationships with your parents.

Talk to a professional, a guidance counselor or a trusted TruBlue as soon as possible if you feel something isn't healthy with your parental relationship.

Establishing Healthy Dating Relationships

Healthy TruBlue and parent relationships are essential to being the Total Package Girl. But what about when you date? Do you know how to make solid choices in your one-on-one relationship? What if it doesn't feel healthy? Then what? And how do you know if you are a good match with someone? How do you exit a negative relationship?

Dating Assessment Guide

If you are questioning your relationship, ask yourself:

❋ *Is this person healthy for me? (If you can't answer this with a resounding yes, then it's a no.)*

❋ *Am I really excited to be with this person because this person is genuinely nice to me and makes my spirit soar?*

❋ *Does this person have healthy or unhealthy habits? If unhealthy, does this person try to push bad habits onto me?*

* How do I rate this person's quality of character, ethics, and responsibility on a scale of 1 to 5, with 5 being the highest level of responsibility?

* Does this person's value system of honesty, integrity, trust, mutual love and respect, and faithfulness align with mine? (See Secret Weapon #3 for a list of core values.)

* Am I keeping this person in my life only because I'm afraid to leave due to safety concerns?

* Am I staying in this relationship because I'm too nice to leave and don't want to hurt this person's feelings?

* Do I have fun and laugh with this person?

* Does this person bring out the best in me?

CAUTIONARY NOTE!

If you've answered these questions sincerely and ranked this person low on any one of these questions, it's time to reassess the relationship status.

Is a little voice inside you screaming that this relationship is wrong? Be courageous, face facts, deal directly with the situation, move on, or seek professional or TruBlue assistance to do so. You deserve an awesome, healthy relationship.

Know and Love Yourself

Total Package Girl Secret Weapon #3 is awesome because when you know and love yourself, everything is more fun. You're confident, you go for what you want, and life is more fulfilling. Fun and fulfilling— what a combination! With this secret weapon, you feel good about yourself, and you aren't as afraid to try new adventures, meet new people, and stretch your goals.

#jbu and not who everyone else tells you to be. Stand up for you and what you believe in.
#StandUp #TotalPackageGirl

Loving yourself doesn't mean you are conceited or a bragger. It means you are really happy with who you are. And it's not as difficult as you might think.

Learning to Know and Love Yourself

 Make #SmartChick Choices to Gain Self-Trust

No doubt, when you make solid decisions and take positive actions, you build trust in yourself. Choices like reading this book are positive and teach you the smart life lessons and secret weapons of the Total Package Girl early in life. This gives you long-term benefits like positive energy, more fun, and the ability to reach your dreams.

When life gets challenging, be confident and trust yourself to make smart choices. When your parents tell you to "make good choices" as you are running out the door for a party, that means they foresee decisions you may face that could greatly impact your future—for better or for worse. And they know that making right choices at a party takes you down a completely different path than making wrong choices at a party. Remember the soccer coach?

 Listen to Your Inner Voice

If you quiet your outside voice, sometimes you'll hear your inner voice chattering with you. That's your Total Package Girl intuition making itself known. For example, if someone is trying to peer-pressure you into smoking marijuana, that's the perfect time to listen to your inner voice because it's probably screaming at you not to do it. Each time you work through tough situations like that, *#LoveYouSomeYou* and celebrate that you just made an amazing choice. Your spirit will soar with confidence. That is why it is so important to listen to and trust your inner voice.

TOTAL PACKAGE GIRL ACTIVITY:
How Well Do I Know My Inner Voice?

My inner voice is always talking to me. If I get really quiet #RightNow, what do I hear it saying?

⭐ I will start training myself to listen more to my inner voice.

Essence (n.)

The basic, real nature or core of an individual.

*Living true to your **essence** gives you freedom and a soaring spirit.*

TOTAL PACKAGE GIRL ACTIVITY:
Knowing My Essence

What do other people see in me? *(Ask them!)*

☐ Happy ☐ Sad ☐ Mean ☐ Kind ☐ Scared

☐ Easy-going ☐ Other: _____

Is this a true picture of the real me? ☐ Yes ☐ No

How could it be closer to the real me?

When people hear my words and see my social media posts, what kind of person would they describe me as?

☐ Appropriate ☐ Risky ☐ Funny ☐ Smart

☐ Nice ☐ Other: _____

Does this portray the true essence of me? ☐ Yes ☐ No

⭐ **My comments about my spoken words and my social media posts:**

Am I portraying the real me to others? ☐ Yes ☐ No

Know What You Stand For

Secret Weapon #3 is all about discovering who you are, inside and out. For example, do you know your core values, talents, and loves? Let's find out.

 Core Values: Your Inner Driver

Core values are your guiding principles. They drive how you think as well as your actions. They are what you feel the strongest about, deep down. They drive who you are, what you believe, what motivates you, and who and what comes into your life.

There are hundreds of core values including:

loyalty	courage	honesty	fairness
achievement	ambition	generosity	optimism
love	respect	fun	kindness
knowledge	freedom	logic	peace
status	happiness	comfort	calmness
fame	discipline	education	curiosity
compassion	integrity	power	truth
spirit	wealth	virtuosity	family

For example, if someone drops money on the floor and you are the only one to see her do it, do you pick up the money and pocket it, thinking "finders keepers," or do you return it to the rightful owner? How you answer depends on whether honesty is a strong core value of yours.

Talents: Your Shining Stars

Your talents are things you are good at naturally. They come easy to you and are your gifts and abilities. Examples may include: photography, playing a musical instrument, nurturing animals, participating in a sport, excelling in an academic subject like math or science, public speaking, writing songs, or drawing.

 Loves: Your Soaring Heart

Your loves are the things, people, or experiences that absolutely make your heart sing. You would do or be there in a heartbeat for the things you love. They make you happy, and you completely adore and enjoy them without question. Examples could be: dancing, writing, music, cats, dogs, horses, swimming, drawing, playing soccer, being with a special person, cooking, or singing.

If you merge your talents with your loves, you will be living out your dreams.

Blend your talents with your loves
to reach your dreams.
#TotalPackageGirlDreams

 TOTAL PACKAGE GIRL ACTIVITY:
How to Blend My Talents and Loves

Use the previous definitions and identify the following:

My talents are:

⭐

⭐

⭐

My loves are:

⭐

⭐

⭐

Be creative and do some soul searching on this one:

What activity, action, or job on this earth could I participate in that would blend my talents with my loves?

SECRET WEAPON #3

TOTAL PACKAGE GIRL ACTIVITY:
Know-Me-Better Quiz

How well do you really know yourself? Here's a fun list of questions to get to know the inner you even better:

Am I talkative or shy in a group?

Am I nervous about speaking up or expressing my opinions?

☐ Yes ☐ No

What are my top four core values? (see page 85)

⭐ ⭐

⭐ ⭐

What qualities do I look for in my friends?

⭐ ⭐

⭐ ⭐

Do I have an open and comfortable relationship with my parents or guardians?

☐ Yes ☐ No

If I have a conflict, do I know how to resolve it?

☐ Yes ☐ No

[88]

TOTAL PACKAGE GIRL ACTIVITY:
Know-Me-Better Quiz (cont'd)

Is there a certain look that I like?
(Examples: Glam, preppy, urban, vintage, classic, earthy, shabby chic, sporty, bold, Goth, elegant, whatever I'm feeling that day)

☐ Yes: _____ ☐ No, not really

Would I help someone I saw being bullied, or would I be afraid to get involved?

☐ Help ☐ Be afraid

Why? _____

What adjectives would I use to describe myself?
(Examples: Confident, worried, achiever, shy, happy, friendly, mean, nice, fun, disciplined, lazy, helpful, sad, quiet, loud, fair, rule-follower, rule-bender, attractive, positive, negative)

⭐ _____ ⭐ _____

⭐ _____ ⭐ _____

List my physical and personality traits and descriptive characteristics.
(Examples: Hair color and length, height, funny, serious)

⭐ Physical: _____

⭐ Personality: _____

TOTAL PACKAGE GIRL ACTIVITY:
Know-Me-Better Quiz (cont'd)

How would I handle someone asking me to smoke, drink, or do drugs?

Am I prepared to stand up for myself if/when others disrespect me? If yes, what will I say?

☐ Yes ☐ No

What is my status on world and social issues?

⭐ Politics:

⭐ Religion:

⭐ Environment:

What do I love most about myself, specific to:

⭐ My Body:

⭐ My Brain:

⭐ My Spirit:

TOTAL PACKAGE GIRL ACTIVITY:
Know-Me-Better Quiz (cont'd)

Am I impressed with others' clothes, possessions, social status, money?

☐ Yes ☐ No

If yes, which ones? _____

Do I brag, gossip or talk about people behind their backs?

☐ Yes ☐ No

Note: If you find yourself doing so, simply acknowledge it, forgive yourself, and begin to take steps to improve the quality of the comments that come out of your mouth. Being aware is the first step.

Am I always truthful, fair, and trustworthy to others?

☐ Yes ☐ No

Do I know what words or actions are not okay in terms of how people treat me?

☐ Yes ☐ No

Write them here:

_____

Do I love myself?

☐ Yes ☐ No

SECRET WEAPON #3

If you don't have answers to all of these quiz questions, no worries. The purpose is to start a conversation and give you a glimpse into yourself like you've probably never had before. *The better you know yourself, the more confident you can be.*

It's fun to get to know yourself better, don't you agree? As you go through this book, remember that your feelings are your feelings. No judgments. They are what they are. And no one can change that—although they may try.

Don't push aside your feelings. They may be based on your past life experiences—fun, happy, sad—and no one has had those exact same experiences. So celebrate and allow your feelings to simply *be.*

Also, expect that your feelings and opinions might change through the years as you grow older and gain more life moments, meet new people, and broaden your horizons.

> *To be yourself in a world that is constantly trying to make you something else is the greatest accomplishment.*
> —*Ralph Waldo Emerson*

Fashion and You

 TOTAL PACKAGE GIRL ACTION:
Explore Style, Just For Fun

When it comes to fashion, you get back what you put out there. Agreed? So think about wearing things that match your feelings, your true personality, your values, and spirit. Think about your own look and style. What do you like to wear? Certain colors? A certain store or brand, or kind of clothing? What type of shoes? What about your hairstyle? Do you like accessories or are you a bit simpler? Are you a bracelet girl, or a glasses, hat, or scarf girl? Do you often wear athletic clothes? Are you most comfortable when you are casual? What about makeup—do you wear it? A little or a lot? Explore that too, just for fun. Remember, it isn't about what it costs, it's about what feels true to you. And of course, the best accessory you have is to **#jbu** with your biggest smile!

TOTAL PACKAGE GIRL ACTIVITY:
Fashion and Me Quiz

Circle one letter for each number to explore what fashion I like:

1. **A.** I love wearing dresses.
   B. I like the casual look.
   C. I like vibrant clothes.
   D. I love scholarly things.

2. **A.** I love to dress up and play princess.
   B. It's important for me to be comfortable.
   C. I like setting myself apart from others in the room.
   D. If it fits well and looks good on me, I'll keep wearing it.

3. **A.** I like lace and soft colors.
   B. I like denim, cotton, and natural fibers.
   C. I love bling, bright accessories, and big jewelry.
   D. Tailored clothes are the best.

4. **A.** I'm a girlie girl: lipstick, nail polish, hair accessories.
   B. No high heels for me.
   C. I like crazy combinations and wild patterns.
   D. I'm okay with simple yet elegant.

5. **A.** I like to look feminine.
   B. I wear very little jewelry, if any.
   C. I probably spend more on clothes than my friends do.
   D. I want to look sleek and timeless; not the latest trend.

TOTAL PACKAGE GIRL ACTIVITY
Fashion and Me Quiz (cont'd)

If you chose mostly **A**, you chose a creative and romantic style.

If you chose mostly **B**, you chose a natural and wholesome style.

If you chose mostly **C**, you chose a trendy and bold style.

If you chose mostly **D**, you chose a classic and sophisticated style.

Did anything surprise you about what you liked? Write it here:

Note: *If you don't have a particular style or look, that's just fine. Explore an individual look in a way that feels fun, natural, and sends the message that brings out the real you (and not what you think someone else wants you to be).*

Describe my own looks and fashion interests here:

SECRET WEAPON #3

Total Package Girls, Stay Strong!

There's an inner power that comes with knowing how you'd handle certain tough situations. Arming yourself with the secret weapon of knowing and loving yourself helps you make solid choices when you truly need to the most.

How Strong Would You Be?

Life brings challenges that require strong choices. How strong would you be if:

* ❋ *Someone gossiped so meanly about you and it was all lies?*

* ❋ *Someone didn't invite you to a party?*

* ❋ *Someone posted unflattering pictures of you online?*

* ❋ *Guys made fun of you and tried to embarrass you regularly?*

* ❋ *Someone told you that you were fat or ugly and should just die?*

* ❋ *Someone asked you to send an inappropriate selfie via text, Snapchat, or other?*

* ❋ *Someone asked you to do drugs, drink alcohol, or participate in another illegal activity?*

Some of the above are actual bully scenarios. Be strong and powerful if you experience these. Protect yourself with love, TruBlues, and your smart brain.

CAUTIONARY NOTE!

Some people throughout life will try to bring you down or make you feel just plain awful—for whatever reason, be it jealously, sheer nastiness, or their own insecurities.

Knowing what to do in those situations will greatly help. So plan ahead, try not to react to negative tactics when possible, and rise above.

Express Your Opinions

When you are confident in your beliefs, it's easier to stand up for yourself and others at school, at a birthday party, at any social event. Conversely, if you don't know where you stand, you risk getting walked on, misjudged, or treated negatively or unfairly by mean girls. You also stand at risk of being bullied, ostracized, and picked on. This is why Secret Weapon #3 is so crucial.

#RightNow, begin the Total Package Girl skill of speaking up. Get in the habit of stating your opinions—of jumping into conversations because you know you have something worthy, relevant, funny, or important to add. Say your opinion when a teacher asks the class to discuss something. If someone asks you what you'd like to do, don't say, "I don't know," but rather, express your thoughts. Don't be afraid to jump in and share them—just do it! As a Total Package Girl, your confidence shines through in your words, and it gets easier to speak up after the first scary time you do it.

Bad Days

Sometimes other people's bad days project onto yours. If you get the "galloping grumps"—those grumpy bad moods and a negative attitude that seem to travel to and from others—practice saying positive things to yourself and about yourself as soon as the grumps hit. Remember, it's okay to have bad days. Another thing to do is to try to understand the root of your grumps. If you know that and can deal with that reason, it may help you move on. This is a powerful way to stay grounded and to honor your feelings.

Research shows that those who know and love themselves are happier and more likely to achieve their goals – more good reasons to be positive.

#MeMantras

Be positive every day by having **#MeMantras**. Here are some good ones from other Total Package Girls to get you started, to perk up your day, to keep your inner girl strong and happy, and to comfort you when you need it. Use these or write your own and add them to the list:

 I'm awesome.

 I love who I am.

My future is amazing.

 It's going to be an amazing day.

 I love me.

 I love my body.

 I'm so smart.

 I'm brilliant.

 I love my freckles (and my nose, my hair, my legs).

 I look amazing.

 I'm totally going to reach my dream.

 I can do it.

 I did it.

 I totally trust me.

 I made a great decision.

 That wasn't easy but I'm proud of me for doing it.

 My life is amazing and fun. I'm so blessed.

 I'm going to make today awesome.

 I'm powerful.

 I'm strong.

 I'm staying positive.

⭐ *Somebody loves me #RightNow.*

⭐ *I am gorgeous inside and out.*

⭐ *I am thankful that I'm me.*

⭐ *I'm really thankful for:* _____

TOTAL PACKAGE GIRL ACTIVITY:
Write My Own #MeMantras

Which mantras do I like the most?
Write them, or any others, here:

_____

_____

_____

Power is in the House

Can you handle meanness when it comes at you or do you absorb it like a sponge absorbs germs? It's tough to be your own powerhouse and to stop letting negativity in. But at those times, remember, you are never powerless.

Picture yourself holding a Power Shield in front of you. Imagine it protecting you from negative influencers, from the evil or mean people in the world. Envision it absorbing all negative comments, actions, and people coming at you, and see it protecting your total package: Body, Brain, and Spirit. Imagine it, too, allowing you to speak up, project, and say just what you believe and exactly how you feel. It's amazingly refreshing, isn't it?

That's what we're talking about! It's your own shield of power and protection. And guess what? You have a Power Shield of your own! **#RightNow**, this very second, you can begin using it.

When people pull you away from the essence of you, turn your positive spirit negative, or treat you poorly, use your Power Shield. It gives you the strength to stay on your Total Package Girl path, be strong, **#jbu**, and let the negative go. Let your Power Shield protect you, attract the positive, and repel any meanness or evil that is trying to influence you. Keep your Power Shield close and never be afraid to use it!

Power comes from within. Take powerful, amazing steps, and do not be afraid.
#TotalPackageGirlPowerShield

Total Package Girl
Power Shield
Protecting Body, Brain, and Spirit

Having your own Power Shield gives you the amazing ability to protect and take care of yourself. Your Power Shield allows you to say, "I will not let others mistreat, control, or act meanly towards me. I will stay strong, powerful, and courageous." It helps you handle the tough moments and say what you mean and need to say.

When people are mean or you feel challenged, here are some Power Shield truths to tell yourself:

 I'm thankful I'm me.

 I'm better than this situation, and I will walk away.

 Tomorrow is a fresh, new day.

 I'm blocking those negative people.

 My feelings are legit.

 I'm not letting that ridiculousness inside my shield. I respect myself too much.

 I will stay ultra-positive and radiate positive energy in this moment.

 I will be positive and compliment myself when I hear negative talk.

 My inner girl voice is powerful. I will speak up.

 It's fine to let go of negative people in my world; if they don't like me for me and have continued to tease me about

things like my acne, my freckles, my clothes, and my life,
I'll choose to walk away and stay close to my TruBlues
instead. I'm moving on from such immature games.

 I will look in the mirror and see my beauty on the
outside, and I'll remind myself of my inner beauty too.

 I will take action by doing healthy, good things for myself,
like downloading the Total Package Lifestyle app for the
best daily #MeMantras to start my day.

Scan this QR code
to get the free
Total Package Lifestyle
app on your
smartphone now!

Activating your Total Package Girl Power Shield means you don't
have to absorb others' negative energy anymore. You get to let in and
project the positive and minimize the negative ... whether that's people
or situations. No doubt words can hurt, but using your Power Shield
takes away some of the sting.

Benefits of Using Your Power Shield

☑ *You get to use your savvy brain to make solid choices, like hanging out with friends whose values match yours.*

☑ *You get to show the world the real and confident you, and you can see TruBlues reveal themselves.*

☑ *You give up worry, trusting the shield's power and the faith you feel inside.*

☑ *You gain power in your actions and block attitudes that hold you back.*

☑ *Your talents and strengths really start to shine.*

☑ *You laugh more and have fun.*

☑ *You deeply love you for you, so when you look in the mirror, you love what you see and feel grounded in who you are.*

☑ *Your strength in discerning good from evil is huge, like knowing TruBlues from mean girls.*

☑ *You feel confident and secure, and you trust your inner Total Package Girl with no fear of making a poor choice, because even if you do, you know how to forgive yourself, learn from it, and move on.*

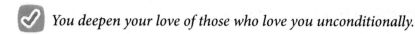 *You deepen your love of those who love you unconditionally.*

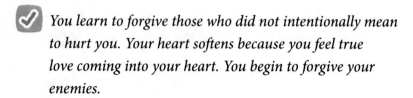 *You learn to forgive those who did not intentionally mean to hurt you. Your heart softens because you feel true love coming into your heart. You begin to forgive your enemies.*

✅ *You gain patience with others and yourself and learn how to work through problems, not to give up or throw in the towel every time adversity comes your way.*

Ah ... clarity, protection, power. Your Power Shield surrounds you like an invisible shell, a safeguard. It's like radar, detecting negative external forces that are trying to deny you your positive energy. Your Power Shield works with your GPS to keep you moving in the right direction, to project positive energy, and to attract those things in life that bring happiness.

The Power Shield helps protect:

BODY	BRAIN	SPIRIT
The Physical You	The Intellectual and Academic You	The Spiritual and Emotional You

Total Package Girl Exit Strategy

Sometimes you get stuck in a really tough situation, whether it's with an anti-TruBlue, a mean girl, or peers pressuring you. That's when you need an exit strategy.

• •

Exit Strategy (n.)

A plan to get you out of a negative situation.

*When you are prepared with an **exit strategy**, peer pressure can be easier to handle.*

• •

Here are ways to implement your very own exit strategy when in a pressure situation:

 Stand strong with your Power Shield. Be firm and directly confront the person pressuring you when possible. Tell this person how you feel. Use solid eye contact, a strong voice, and clear, direct words. Although it may be tough, learn this face-to-face confrontation skill, and you will be grateful you did. Role play with a TruBlue or by yourself in a mirror to build your confidence. Use direct eye contact and say something like, "I don't like the way you treat me" or "You aren't healthy for me/nice to me, so I'd rather not hang out anymore" or simply, "I'm busy" or "I can't" when it comes to hangouts. That lets the person know that you'll no longer take the negativity and that you are proactively choosing to move on or get away from her or him.

2 *Use your parents as an excuse.* "My parents aren't letting me" or "My mom said I have to be home by ten. Gotta go."

3 *Have an out.* Avoid situations where the bully or mean girl will be, when possible. The less your paths cross, the better. But if you do meet up, whether it's in a one-on-one situation or an after-school or evening event, have an out and a reason not to be there if you suspect dangerous or high-risk situations, such as: "My parents need me," "I have relatives in town," or "I'm busy tonight." Keep your TruBlues close when potentially scary or tough situations face you.

Insight: Be a TruBlue to someone else. You may need to help someone else get out of a tough situation as well. Remember that TruBlues are mutual, and if you know how cruddy it feels to be around anti-TruBlues or mean girls, make it a point to be the best TruBlue you can be to someone else.

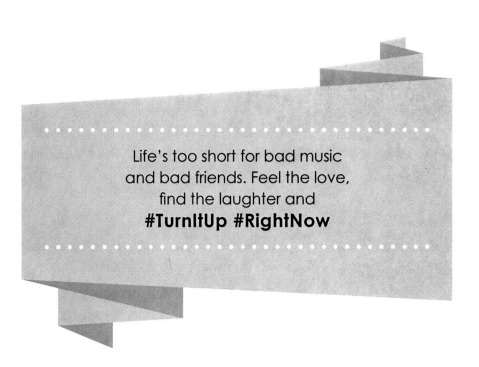

Life's too short for bad music and bad friends. Feel the love, find the laughter and **#TurnItUp #RightNow**

CAUTIONARY NOTE!

Expressing feelings is usually a good thing; however, be careful when putting controversial or deep feelings in writing—such as texts, e-mails, or social media posts. A mean girl may forward your written words to many other people at your expense.

TOTAL PACKAGE GIRL ACTIVITY:
How Strong Will I Be?

Now it's time to test out your strength in these tough situations. First, circle the letter of your opinion:

A. "I will not tolerate this."

B. "I am fine with this."

C. "I don't care either way."

Second, write on the line what you'd say or what your exit strategy would be if that happened to you. Consider #MeMantras and your Power Shield. Once you've written down your comments, practice saying them out loud and role playing. If comfortable, share these actions with a TruBlue.

If someone gossiped so meanly about me and it was all lies:

A　　　**B**　　　**C**

Exit Strategy:

If someone posted unflattering pictures of me:

A　　　**B**　　　**C**

Exit Strategy:

If a guy treated me inappropriately:

A　　　**B**　　　**C**

Exit Strategy:

If someone called me names repeatedly:

A   B   C

Exit Strategy: _____

If someone asked me to send them an inappropriate selfie:

A   B   C

Exit Strategy: _____

If I were being bullied (e.g. if someone told me I should just die):

A   B   C

Exit Strategy: _____

If others were being bullied in front of me:

A   B   C

Exit Strategy: _____

If someone didn't invite me to a party:

A   B   C

Exit Strategy: _____

If I got caught posting something inappropriate online:

A   B   C

Exit Strategy: _____

If I were asked to drink, smoke, or do drugs:

A   B   C

Exit Strategy: _____

The tough issues in the previous activity are serious and not to be taken lightly. If any of these things have happened to you and you feel you truly need help with them, seek out a professional, a teacher or administrator, a parent, or a TruBlue who can help you navigate these tough waters so you don't have to go through it alone. It's courageous to get the help you need.

Imagine Your Future Self

Secret Weapon #3 allows you to see your dreams and future more clearly, whether your "future" is in one day, one week, one month, one year, or one decade.

Imagination becomes reality
with focus and hard work.
#RightNow

Imagine your future self smiling and happy, living out your amazing dreams. Imagine positive future actions in your life, such as the following:

 A fun career you've always wanted to pursue

 A happy family life

 Meeting your personal goals

 Good friends and healthy relationships

 A rockin', energetic, fit, and healthy body, and a confident you, not worried about physicality

 A happy, positive person with an amazing respect and love of self

 A person who shows love, gives back, and treats others with respect and kindness ... and receives it right back

 A brilliant person who has TruBlues by her side and doesn't have to try too hard to fit in ... #jbu

 A person who makes good choices (regarding such things as peers and social media)

TOTAL PACKAGE GIRL ACTIVITY:
Defining My Dreams and Future Self

What are my dreams?

What does success mean to me now and in my future?

Set Your Total Package Girl Goals

Ever shoot archery? What if there were no target? How would you know where to aim?

Now, what if you had no target—no goals—in life? You might wander aimlessly day after day and feel lost and directionless. This is a good example of why you need to set legit goals for yourself. Otherwise, you are taking steps on a road that leads to nowhere, with no target and no GPS.

Goals are the dreams you wish to achieve. Bring your "A" game everywhere you go and watch your dreams come to life.
#TotalPackageLifestyle

Knowing where you'd like to be in one year, five years, and ten years is a great way to start goal-setting. It helps you take one step at a time. That way, your goals stick, you know the target you are aiming for, and you have a greater chance of seeing your dreams come true. And, of course, you can adjust your goals as life changes (because it will).

Goals help you stay focused and on your Total Package Girl path. They are the target of your GPS, keeping you on a path that's just right for you.

TOTAL PACKAGE GIRL ACTIVITY:
My Total Package Girl Goals

Fill in the following Total Package Girl activity with your short- and long-term goals. Include dreams, accomplishments, career, family— and of course, your Body, Brain, and Spirit.

In *one* year, I'd like to be:

In *five* years, I'd like to be:

In *ten* years, I'd like to be:

When I am one hundred years old, looking back on my life, what would I like it to look like?

*For more advice and tips on goal-setting, get our Total Package Professional tool at **www.TotalPackageGirl.com***

Develop Rockin' Communication Skills

Ever been misunderstood? When someone took what you said, got it all wrong, and then got mad at you? Or falsely spread a rumor about something you never said?

Well, Total Package Girl Secret Weapon #4 helps you rock your words and your actions and keep those misunderstandings to a minimum. It allows you to speak words that come from the inner true you, to more clearly express your opinions and thoughts, and to effectively communicate what the real you is all about.

. . . .

Communicate (v.)

To effectively transmit, share and understand thoughts and feelings so that the intended message sent is the message received.

*When I **communicate**, I will clearly speak up and use my true voice to express my opinions.*

. . . .

No one can put words in your mouth
or speak for you. Your words matter.
#BeTheTotalPackageGirl #StandUp

This secret weapon arms you with the skills you need to clearly get your message across to other people with little or no confusion. Sounds much easier than it really is!

Ever say something that you think is just a random comment and someone takes your words the wrong way and doesn't talk to you for days, even weeks? That's a great example of the communication process breaking down.

We all want people to "get" what we are saying so they pick up what we're puttin' down. That's always the goal, but not always the real deal.

Every time you speak, you have a message you want to get across to someone, right? That makes you the sender, and the person to whom you are speaking is the receiver. There are many other variables involved in communication though. For example, talking on the phone is different than talking in person or video-chatting. When you can't see the sender, it changes things.

The Differences Between Verbals and Nonverbals

Verbal communication: what is spoken, the things you say, your actual words.

Nonverbal communication: includes body language, gestures, and all things affecting the message other than the spoken words.

To be a great Total Package Girl communicator, you need to know how effective you are at both verbal and nonverbal communication. No doubt about it, without effective communication skills, expressing yourself accurately is impossible. For example, if someone were smoking a cigarette, eating a jumbo order of curly fries, drinking a sugar-laden soda, *and* at the same time talking about being fit and healthy, which would you believe—the actions or the words? The nonverbals cancel out the verbals, don't you agree?

People form an opinion of you from the moment they first see you. They learn a lot about you in the first few seconds. You've heard the expression "First impressions count." They do, and will continue to throughout your whole life. Research shows that 90 percent of opinions are formed within the first twenty seconds of meeting someone. As another expression says, "You only get one chance to make a first impression."

TOTAL PACKAGE GIRL EXAMPLE:
The Interview

Without clear communication and a professional appearance, an interviewee has little chance of getting the job. For example, if an interviewee chews gum, wears torn clothing, and texts during the interview, nonverbal communication indicates that this person is either not interested in getting the job or is not a solid representative for the company. If the interviewee swore or told stories that were off-topic and unrelated to the job she was interviewing for, she likely would not get the job because her verbal communication wasn't effective or on point.

In almost every case, companies would rather not hire and continue looking for a job candidate than hire someone who would seemingly be a bad fit for the job or company. So pay attention to both your verbals and nonverbals; it's important to know how others perceive you.

What could the interviewee above have done differently to change the perception and give herself a better opportunity to get the job?

Insight: If you find that people often don't understand what you are saying, take a deep dive and analyze both your verbal and nonverbal skills. They made need sharpening.

● ●

Your Nonverbals Speak the Loudest

What you *don't* say is as important as what you *do* say. Nonverbals, some say, represent up to 90 percent of communication and include your body language and actions but not your words. Nonverbals include:

 Proximity. This is about personal space. How close do you stand to others when you talk with them? Do you invade their space or stand far away? Beyond approximately eighteen inches is considered comfortable communication distance for the average person. Ever have a stranger get right up next to you when talking—like inches away from your face? It's very uncomfortable, isn't it?

 Posture. Do you stand tall or slouch? Are your shoulders back or rounded? Are your arms or legs crossed? Is your head tilted or straight up and down? Rounded shoulders and head hanging down can exude low self-esteem. Good posture matters.

 Clothing and makeup. Are you neat or sloppy? Do you use too much makeup or perhaps not enough? Dress for the environment and invest in a nice interview outfit. (Get our Total Package Professional online course for details on dressing for success at work!)

Facial expressions. Are yours positive or negative? Do you nod, wink, roll your eyes? Is your brow furrowed? What about your lips—are they pursed together? Do you frown often or smile a lot? Don't let facial expressions get distracting, but let them show interest and positive feedback.

 Eye contact. Where do you look when talking with someone—at the ground, around the room, or in their eyes? For example, looking away for extended periods shows low interest or the inability to focus. That's why teachers can immediately tell which students are engaged in their classroom discussions and which ones aren't. Conversely, staring without blinking is awkward ... zoning out, perhaps? Make solid eye contact.

 Sounds. Do you clear your throat repeatedly, laugh loudly, or giggle nervously? These sounds could be signs of immaturity, awkwardness, or lack of confidence. Keep sounds to a minimum to lessen distractions.

 Hand gestures. How much do you move your hands when you talk? Do you fidget, wring your hands, tap your fingers, or touch other people when you talk with them? These may be distracting. Keep these controlled.

Why pay attention to nonverbals? Because they say a lot about you and how the world perceives you, and they can get in the way of your message being heard and received. Nonverbals can tell a complete stranger how confident you are; if you have high, low, or no self-esteem; if you are open and communicative; if you are unapproachable or shy; and even if you want the job or don't really care about it.

Give yourself a greater chance to win the class election, get the job, or earn the promotion, by knowing and improving your nonverbal style to get the most out of first impressions and future opportunities. This could mean the difference between being bullied or being respected, between getting the internship or losing it. You don't want to close the door before it's even opened.

Other Factors That Affect Communication

Ever try to tell someone something at a concert? It's impossible to hear anything other than the loud music, let alone have your message clearly understood. Noisy environments can contribute to miscommunication.

Also, the time of day is relevant to effective communication. For example, if you are talking to someone at midnight and they are super tired, they may not be hearing or comprehending what you are saying to them. Ever have someone call you first thing in the morning before you are even awake? You barely remember what day it is, let alone what they are saying to you. In these examples, if you consider the time of day, no wonder the message wasn't accurately received.

Know your communication style and improve wherever you can. Something as simple as looking at the floor when you talk, or using "um" or "like" to the extreme, can keep someone from taking you seriously. Having rockin' communication skills is an amazing secret weapon you will always have—at school, at work, in relationships, in life. It's a gift that keeps on giving! **#TotalPackageGirl**

TOTAL PACKAGE GIRL ACTIVITY:
What Do My *Verbals* Tell Others?

Check out your verbal communication skills. In addition to answering these questions yourself, you may want to have a little fun with this activity and ask others about your communication skills. See how their answers vary from your own.

Am I a slow or fast talker? Am I a loud or soft talker?

Do I come across as serious or funny?

Do I articulate my words or am I a bit of a mumbler?

Do I speak intelligently, or do I exaggerate and tell dramatic or long-winded stories?

Do I speak concisely, or do I ramble and use words like "um" or "like" often?

Assess what you just learned about yourself.
What do I do well when I speak? Where can I improve?

TOTAL PACKAGE GIRL ACTIVITY:
What Do My *Nonverbals* Tell Others?

Now, think about your nonverbals. Self-assess or ask others, then write down poor, average, or super to describe your status in the listed areas. Rank yourself 1 – 5, with 5 being highly effective and 1 needing improvement. Then, work to improve where needed—no judgments allowed!

	poor/average/super	1 to 5
proximity		
posture		
clothing		
makeup		
body language		
facial expressions		
eye contact		
sounds		
hand gestures		

Three Communication Styles

There are three categories of communication style that Total Package Girls need to be aware of. Style relates to how you approach your overall conversations.

Do you go directly at people with a loud voice or opinion before they have a chance to express themselves? Do you beat around the bush or get quiet in a confrontation, not saying what you truly feel? Are you somewhere in the middle? Whatever your style is, it's important to realize that different people and situations may bring out different styles in you. For example, if someone is accusing you of something, you may become more aggressive and loud because you need to stand up for yourself. Or you may do the opposite—get very quiet and shut down because you are nervous or intimidated.

Three communication styles to consider are:

1 *Passive.* Passive communication may mean being quiet, saying nothing, and shutting down when conflict arises. This style can be interpreted as ineffective, weak, unintelligent, or shy. With passive communication, you may fear standing up or being heard, or expressing your opinion. You might be passive in your communication because you don't know the people you are talking to very well, you aren't comfortable speaking in front of others, you don't know where you stand on what is being discussed, or you have little confidence. A timid student who never speaks in class would be a passive communicator.

2 *Aggressive.* This communication style intimidates others because it involves threatening body language; loud, strong, or abrasive words; yelling; finger-pointing; accusations; or very strong opinions. This style can be interpreted as being overbearing, out of control, immature, or a "loose cannon." You may have experienced certain coaches using this style.

3 *Assertive.* This is the acceptable and preferred style of communication in most cases. Assertive communication is typically solution-oriented and respectful, with a steady, even-keeled voice, making it easier to get to the end result— effective receipt of the message. Being assertive makes people feel comfortable. It is a respectful way to talk to others and articulate an opinion so you are better understood. A re-elected mayor may possess the assertive style.

Style #3 allows for the entire communication process to work most effectively. When using the assertive style, the words "I feel" or "I need" can help, especially when you really need someone to hear your point, such as with parents. Remember that some people are terrible listeners, and you may need to tell them more than once.

Insight: Don't give up if you have a very important point to make and the receiver isn't listening. Keep trying, using "I feel" language. Let the person you are talking to know just how vital and important to you this information is.

Tone in the Spoken and Written Word

Think pitch (high or low) and volume (loud or soft) when it comes to tone in your spoken words. Even pets notice your tone; if you asked your dog, "Did you pee on the carpet?" in a fun, high-pitched, playful voice, your dog would be very happy and ready to play. Yell those same words in a mean voice, and your dog would notice the tone and possibly cower in the corner. Aim for the appropriate pitch and volume when communicating to get a desirable result.

In written communication, remember that there are no facial expressions or tones of voice to use for interpretation. Every time you text, e-mail, blog, or post without a visual (such as a photo or video), what you say may not be received the same way you intended it.

For example, pretend the following is a text to you. Notice the difference in meaning based on what word is in bold:

"**I** found your money!"

"I **found** your money!"

"I found **your** money!"

"I found your **money!**"

In written communication, there's no way to know which of these is correct. Be aware that others may not know which meaning you were referring to. Using an emoji may help to clarify your intent or emotion.

Be careful, too, in your use of punctuation. A popular sentence to make this point is "I just ate, Grandpa," which has a completely different meaning without the comma: "I just ate Grandpa."

When you text or post anything on social media, it's there for the world to see. As you well know, people can easily forward, re-tweet, or take a screenshot of anything you post. Use good judgment by not putting private information, secrets, deep feelings, gossip, or mean comments in writing. (You shouldn't be doing the latter two anyway!) Not everyone has good judgment when it comes to keeping your secrets private.

Remember, rather than pouring your heart out in writing to someone you don't trust, make a phone call or have a face-to-face talk. Likewise, when you are re-tweeting or favoriting, make sure you are making quality choices. A United States senator got in hot water for favoriting an inappropriate tweet. In a related example, if a schoolteacher were to tweet a student's confidential grades, he or she would be making a poor choice. Be savvy not only about the content of your posts but also about favoriting and re-tweeting.

TOTAL PACKAGE GIRL ACTIVITY:
My Tone

Check out your spoken and written word tones.

What is my usual tone of voice? Is it upbeat, high-pitched, happy, under control, clear, friendly, mean, mumbled, or loud? *Describe it here using three or four adjectives.*

☐   ☐

☐   ☐

Are there things I can improve upon to be clearer in my written or spoken words? *If yes, what are they?*

Spoken:

Written:

What communication style do I use most?

☐ Passive   ☐ Aggressive   ☐ Assertive

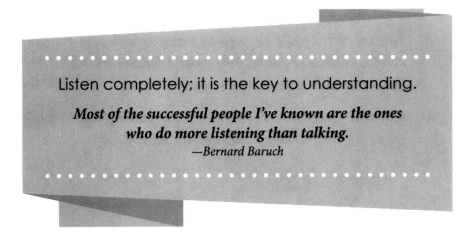

Listen completely; it is the key to understanding.

Most of the successful people I've known are the ones who do more listening than talking.
—Bernard Baruch

Listening Rocks!

You're not alone if, while someone is telling you a story, your attention drifts to your upcoming vacation, what you're having to eat after school, or who you're meeting this weekend. Having amazing listening skills will take you a long way in life. So listen up, Total Package Girl! Learn to be an amazing listener with these tips on what to do and what not to do:

❋ *It's not cool to text while someone is talking to you. Stay focused and put the phone down.*

❋ *It's not okay to constantly interrupt. Be quiet and hear the other person's words.*

❋ *It's not appropriate to "top" a story that someone else is sharing with a better one of yours. Let the person share a story and listen without interrupting.*

❋ *Mirror others' thoughts with comments like, "I hear you ..." or "If I understand what you just said, you are telling me that ..."*

✳   *Give the person you're having a conversation with your complete attention—no walking around, looking around, or doing busywork while the other person is talking.*

✳   *Give others some feedback while they are speaking, such as solid eye contact and a periodic and appropriate nod.*

Communication and Conflict

Ever found yourself in a verbal disagreement or war of words with someone? The words came out wrong and you said something you didn't mean to say (or maybe you did mean it at the time). Feelings get hurt.

When you feel such strong emotions, it's tough to choose smart, productive words to express yourself. After a verbal disagreement, it may be awkward to see that person again, or to apologize as necessary. Uncomfortable, conflict-oriented situations are going to happen. Here are some steps to help you during times of verbal conflict:

✓   ***Try your very best not to yell or raise your voice.*** Doing so makes everyone feel uncomfortable, and yelling puts others on the defensive immediately. (Remember the aggressive communication style?) Try counting to ten or taking deep breaths before speaking.

✓   ***Prepare ahead of time what you are going to say.*** This may not always be possible, but the more prepared the better when it comes to a confrontation.

✓ *Try using the "I feel" technique.* Focusing on your perceptions rather than accusations will make the other person more willing to hear what you have to say. It also helps to tone down high emotions and conflict.

✓ *Think about relevant points you need to get across.* Have a goal in mind to resolve the problem. When all is said and done, what solution are you aiming for?

✓ *Stand your ground.* Be strong and be courageous. Know your side of the issue, and don't let others pull you out of your own thoughts. Articulate your side of the situation. Make solid eye contact and state your opinions firmly, but be reasonable and listen to the other person.

✓ *Be sure this discussion is necessary.* Identify early in the conflict whether or not you are dealing with a person who is merely picking a fight for no reason. Walk away if the person is only looking for conflict. You cannot reason out an imagined problem.

✓ *Minimize the possibility of future conflicts.* Resolve the disagreement if at all possible. Sometimes you may need to "agree to disagree," and that's okay.

✓ *Run your race to the best of your ability.* You can't change the past or accept responsibility for what others have done. You can only do your best to act as nobly as possible in what you've said or done. Accept responsibility for *your* stuff.

Remember that tomorrow is a new day. "This too shall pass" and the sun will come up again. Hard as conflict may be sometimes, forgive yourself and accept the situation for what it is. Learn from it, let it go, and move on. Writing down the lessons you learned from the conflict will help you get back to your Total Package Girl path. **#TPJournalIt** (Get a Total Package Girl Journal and journal it.)

Expressing Anger

We all experience anger in our lives, but ideally not often. It's a signal to us that something is wrong, something needs to change, something isn't sitting well. That's not always bad. When we do have those moments when angry feelings escalate, it's important to express that anger and get those feelings out as productively as possible. Some negative ways people express anger are:

* *Criticizing others with mean or curse words in person or on social media*

* *Screaming and yelling obscenities*

* *Chiding and hurtful teasing, or ganging up on someone, followed by, "Can't you take a joke?"*

* *Getting revenge, such as "I'll get even with her"*

* *Creating a "cold war" with the other person*

* *Hitting someone*

TOTAL PACKAGE GIRL ACTIVITY:
How Do I Express Anger?

Have I used any of the previous negative ways to express anger in the past?

⬜ Yes ⬜ No

Which ones?

_____

Were there better ways for me to express my anger?

⬜ _____ ⬜ _____

⬜ _____ ⬜ _____

⬜ _____ ⬜ _____

CAUTIONARY NOTE!

If you find yourself repeatedly angry or wanting to consistently act in a negative way, please don't be afraid to talk with a trustworthy adult, a TruBlue, or a professional. Likewise, if you are the object of someone's anger, seek immediate professional help for safety's sake.

SECRET WEAPON #4

Successful people do
what others will not ... Be brave.

#TotalPackageGirl

When Angry, Look to Resolve, Not React

When someone has treated you or a loved one poorly, your first thought might be to get defensive, perhaps fight back. Total Package Global is an advocate for standing up for yourself, but in a productive way. Knowing and addressing why you are angry in the first place allows you to minimize or avoid things in the future that trigger your anger.

For example, screaming at the top of your lungs may feel good for releasing the anger in the moment when someone did something hurtful, but it doesn't typically do much on the productive side of things. Why? Because you didn't resolve the situation, you only reacted to it. Determining why something hurt and how you will handle your anger if it happens again is important.

Often those who are intentionally mean are looking for a reaction from you, and the stronger your reaction, the more fuel for their fire.

Don't ignite that flame. Here are some productive suggestions when an angry or confrontational situation occurs:

✅ *Slow your brain down* by taking deep breaths.

✅ *Get to the big picture.* What's going on here and how did this situation happen? What triggered the anger?

✅ *Ask "me" questions* like "Why am I so upset right now?" "How does this affect me or my loved one?" "Is this my fault?" "Am I super-tired and is that why this is bothering me?"

✅ *Ask "them" questions* like "Did this person do it intentionally?" "Is this a pattern from the other person?" "Why would they do this?" "Why are they mad?"

✅ *Assess timing.* Is this the right time to talk about the issue or are tempers too high? Should you walk away from the situation and address it another time? If safety is an issue, remove yourself from the environment and get a responsible adult in the loop so you can handle it with appropriate guidance. You never want to put yourself in physical danger.

✅ *Acknowledge the solution.* How would you like this situation to be resolved? How do you keep it from happening again?

✅ *Do something positive and productive to lessen the anger*, remembering that you cannot control how someone else may react, only how you do. Punch a pillow; talk to the person involved and productively address wrongful actions; apologize and accept responsibility when appropriate; remove yourself from the situation; **#TPJournalIt**.

 Understand that the other person's behavior may continue even after you've confronted this individual in a productive way. That's when you need to pull away, walk away, stay away. Confrontational people may have other issues, such as jealousy or low self-esteem, which are revealed by bringing drama into their world and now yours. They may thrive on this behavior and not respond well to reasoning. Treating others poorly may be their way of feeling better about themselves, but it doesn't have to be yours. Unfortunately, these people may repeatedly use sharp tongues, nasty physical acts, or pranks. Do not accept this kind of negative behavior. Walk away and keep away from environments where confrontations repeatedly occur.

 *Insight:* Work hard to *not* shut down. Do not let the anger go unresolved. It is important to address the problem sooner rather than later, so that you can let the anger go. Keeping it pent up inside of you is super-stressful and unhealthy.

Here are some Total Package Girl techniques to turn those negative feelings around and productively manage anger:

 Breathe. Train yourself to take three slow deep breaths at the time the angry feeling hits you.

 Channel it through exercise. Go for a run, walk, bike ride, do a kick-boxing class.

 Get into nature. Walk through a garden or park.

 Clean up your room, the house, your grandmother's yard.

 #TPJournalIt and write down your feelings.

 Talk productively and directly with the person of conflict.

 Call a TruBlue.

 See a counselor if necessary. This can be extremely healthy and productive in helping you get back to your Total Package Girl path.

Knowing how to handle anger productively is a vital Total Package Girl skill that you will use your entire life. Remember, respond productively and don't just react. Your goal in angry situations is to not let the anger take over or control you, but to ultimately find a solution, learn from it, and move on as quickly as possible. It's okay to feel angry. It's how you channel that anger in a productive fashion, and how you resolve the situation, that matters most. (See your Emotion Checker in Part III for more.)

TOTAL PACKAGE GIRL ACTIVITY:
Expressing Anger Constructively

Are there people or situations I am dealing with now that make me angry?

☐ Yes ☐ No

List them:

☐ _____

☐ _____

☐ _____

☐ _____

What are some ways I can express anger in a healthy way?

☐ Exercise ☐ Talk it out

☐ Punch a pillow ☐ #TPJournalIt

☐ Other:

_____

_____

Trust (v.)

To rely on, have confidence in, believe in.

Trust yourself to make solid choices because you have your Total Package Girl Secret Weapons working for you.

Your Hidden Skills

At some point in your life, you will likely be living on your own, making your own decisions and figuring things out by yourself. That's a big responsibility, and you need every Total Package Girl Secret Weapon to assist. You already possess some pretty amazing life skills, having been through your fair share of life experiences. Here are some examples of the life decisions you make and the skills you already possess:

 You choose your friends.

 You choose the clothes you wear.

 You figure out dramatic situations on your own every day.

 You handle disagreements with your parents, friends, and teammates.

 You make social media, text, or e-mail decisions—your parents aren't always there to guide every app you download or every message you send.

You responsibly turn in your schoolwork.

 You study for tests and earn your own grades. Your grades reflect the effort you've put in.

 You complete responsibilities at home.

 You practice and even train for the sports and activities you participate in.

 You choose to stand up for a person in need.

Because of the inner secret weapons you already possess, realize just how much you can trust yourself. Give yourself credit and don't be afraid to stand up.

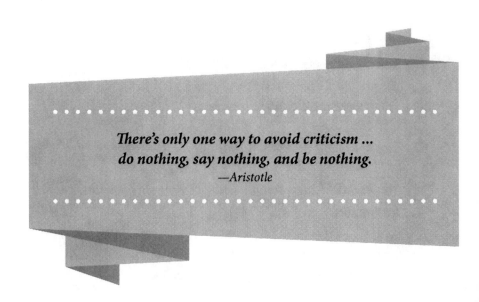

There's only one way to avoid criticism ...
do nothing, say nothing, and be nothing.
—*Aristotle*

 # Aim for Awesome

Living a life of excellence and awesomeness is no small task. Plenty of people walk around with their eyes shut or their heads in the sand, too busy, self-absorbed, or preoccupied to pay attention to the world around them. They think, "I don't have time for that" or "What's in it for me?"

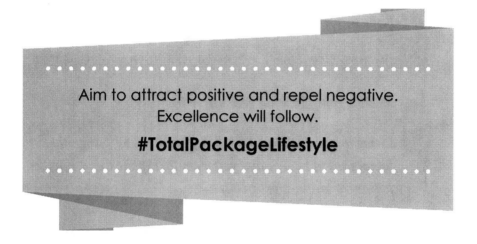

Aim to attract positive and repel negative.
Excellence will follow.
#TotalPackageLifestyle

The Total Package Girl seeks excellence. She goes above and beyond; moves from average to excellent; thinks outside of herself. That's why she has the amazing aura she has, why people really like her, and why she is able to achieve her dreams. When no one is looking, she's helping another, picking up trash, or learning a new skill—because she wants to be a better person, not to be popular or earn recognition. Her motives are pure.

What Awesomeness and Excellence Are

To use Total Package Girl Secret Weapon #5, understand what it means to be awesome and excellent. Authors, theologians, and bloggers often write on the topic of excellence, with each having her or his own opinion on its true meaning. Setting your GPS on awesomeness and excellence means:

- *Doing the right thing when no one is around or watching*

- *Watching and then emulating people who are kind and happy*

- *Being the best at what you do—through hard work and effort; being up for the challenge*

- *Blending talents and loves to make a difference in the world*

- *Steadily going for what you believe in*

- *Living to give back to others; being kind, not for recognition or for an award, but because you want to help the cause, another person, or a situation be better*

- *Leaving it better than you found it*

- *Doing right, especially when wrong seems better, more fun, and more popular*

- *Being dream- and goal-oriented*

- *Leading your own life decisions, not following others'*

- ☑ *When someone asks you to do A, B, and C, doing A, B, C, D, E, F, and G*

- ☑ *Knowing your strengths and working hard to build on them*

- ☑ *Knowing your weaknesses and working hard to improve them*

- ☑ *Doing what you love and being with whom you love (**Note:** Love makes your heart dance—that's how you'll know when you are in the right space and with the right people.)*

What Awesome and Excellent *Aren't*

There are those walking on this planet living life with their eyes closed, looking out only for themselves, never understanding or looking for ways to be humble, kinder, or more loving. They don't offer help to someone who has asked for it and they ignore the people in life who are less fortunate, not wanting to be bothered. These people are not seeking awesomeness or excellence.

More Ways To Be Awesome

The Total Package Girl is surrounded by excellence, primarily because she gets back what she puts out there. She has a unique mindset that isn't all about herself and her ego. That's pretty tough to do in a world where many girls one-up each other and compare their latest technologies and styles, cars, houses, and on and on, in an exhausting fashion.

How do you—the Total Package Girl—stay awesome in an average world? Here's how:

- ✅ ***Create your own true path.*** Don't follow the hype, the media stigma, or what everyone else is doing.

- ✅ ***When you think you're done with a project, a job, a workout,*** do five minutes more.

- ✅ ***When you see a weak link—someone struggling, someone being made fun of—stop and help.*** Don't hesitate to do good for others, especially when they are in need. Look for ways to help. Pick others up when they're down. Don't be surprised if that person you just picked up lends *you* a hand. Your positive ways will pay off.

- ✅ ***When someone kicks you when you're down, don't hate them.*** Get up, move on, and let it make you stronger the next time.

- ✅ ***Shine brighter when you interact with others.*** Smile more; do a little extra something for them. Follow up on a conversation you've had with them. Offer them a compliment. Do an unexpected favor for them.

- ✅ ***Be generous and kind when no one is looking and when no one asks you to*—**something as simple as picking up a pen or a book someone dropped or getting the mail for an elderly neighbor. These random acts of kindness will make someone's day a little brighter.

- ✅ *Let go of past negative experiences* by taking the lessons learned from them and turning them into a positive action.

- ✅ *If you've lost a game, be a gracious loser.* When others succeed, be happy for them, hard as that can be.

- ✅ *Step it up and look for opportunities to make yourself, your talents, or your skills better,* to help more, to achieve more, and to seize the chances that may quietly show up in front of you—such as noticing and helping a disabled person at the supermarket or picking up papers that your teacher dropped.

Insight: When aiming for awesomeness, you will encounter incredible people and experience amazing life moments like never before. Watch it start happening as you aim for awesome.

. . . .

Excel (v.)

To shine, be outstanding, to exceed.

*Make it part of your essence to **excel** in all you do, to make a difference in your world, to be awesome.*

. . . .

Awesomeness at Tough Times

Sounds strange, but your biggest lessons in life are those that are absolutely the pits to go through. The hardest days, the worst drama, the most embarrassing situation, the toughest challenge, your meanest encounter, your biggest heartbreak, a nasty BFF fight, an epic test failure—these times are some of the greatest peak learning moments of your life and actually can lead to awesomeness, *if* you don't miss the lesson they are teaching you.

You won't necessarily see your growth right then, while the ugly stuff is happening, because you are feeling the pain of it. It's only afterward, or when a similar situation happens and you know how to handle it better, that you realize you can be awesome the next time. It is then that you see how far you've come and how much you've grown.

It's About the High Road, Girls

Positivity breeds awesomeness so keep setting (and resetting) your GPS to "positive." Mean girls and tough stuff aren't going to occur every minute of every day of your life. Train your mind to walk on the sunny side of the street, not the rainy one; to focus on being better, not on getting sucked into the negative. When you get a bad grade on a project, don't think your life is over and you stink. Think of the opportunity to improve it on the very next project.

We could all walk around like Eeyore in *Winnie the Pooh*—remember him? He always said in the glummest of voices, "Looks like rain." Research shows that negativity can lead to higher stress and lower self-esteem so train yourself **#RightNow** to be positive and increase your odds of a healthier lifestyle at the same time. **#TotalPackageLifestyle**

When someone insults you about something you are wearing, laugh it off and make a funny comment back. We could all spend our whole lives saying "Did you hear what she said to me?" or "Who does she think she is?" every time someone throws an insult our way. We also could scheme about ways to "get back" at the offender. But rather than that, respond with, "Ha—you gotta love vintage shirts, huh?" That keeps you from being sucked into the negative zone and trains your brain to keep potentially negative interactions more positive, with humor in this case. Remember, people who readily sling negative comments at others are looking for a reaction. Don't give it to them. Take the high road and rise above the negative.

Getting Back to the Ultimate You

When certain people or days pull you out of your positive mode and take you down grumpy street, here are some actions to get you back to the ultimate, more positive you:

 Put on your favorite music and dance.

 Play a musical instrument.

 Watch a funny DVD and laugh.

 Call or text an old friend.

 Do a nice thing for another person.

 Remind yourself of Dorothy and your own ruby slippers.

 Ride a bike or do something physical.

 Spend time with your pet.

 Lay on your bed and daydream.

There's always a new day and a nice person waiting to greet you around the next corner. Focus on that when tough life situations hit you and pull you off your Total Package Girl path like a strong magnetic force. Train yourself to take the high road and to be positive, particularly if you are used to sulking, having pity parties, or creating a bit of drama. Once positivity becomes a habit, you'll be hooked!

TOTAL PACKAGE GIRL ACTIVITY: **Achieving Awesomeness**

When I need to get back to awesome, what do I like to do?

☐ Play with a pet   ☐ Listen/dance to music

☐ Read   ☐ Talk to a TruBlue

☐ Exercise   ☐ Other: _____

Who in my life do I like to be around at tough times because they make me feel awesome?

⭐ _____   ⭐ _____

⭐ _____   ⭐ _____

How can I be awesome every day?

⭐ _____   ⭐ _____

⭐ _____   ⭐ _____

TOTAL PACKAGE GIRL ACTIVITY:
Visualize My Awesome Life

Develop your very own visual image of the amazing, awesome you.

What does the excellent, amazing, and awesome me look like?
(Describe or draw your actions, looks, personality, life.)

When making choices every day, whether at school or at the weekend football game, think about your Total Package Girl life path and ask, "Where am I going, and is this decision or action pointing me in that awesome direction?" You always have options—for right turns, left turns, U-turns, or dead ends. Use your sharpest brain to make the clearest, strongest, most awesome choices you can at that **#RightNow** moment, and live out Total Package Girl Secret Weapon #5 today.

PART III
Absolute Reality

Absolute Reality Check: Life's Tough, Real Stuff

Spoiler alert: Hard stuff happens throughout life. Whether it's an embarrassing moment, a sickness that is all-consuming, or a mean-girl situation, know that these "absolute realities" will occur once in a while and that you will get through them.

• •

Absolute Reality (n.)

The real deal, no sugar-coating; the bare-bones stuff; the good with the bad; the pure, no-filter circumstances in life, life happening without rose-colored glasses.

Absolute reality is cut-to-the-chase truth, when you are all alone in your thoughts, looking at your life as it is—honestly.

• •

You can't control your DNA or your family. You also can't control certain life events that come your way unexpectedly. Part of getting through these rough spots is being prepared for potentially stressful times. Following is a list of some tough realities life can serve up. Ever have any of the following things happen to you? If you haven't, this is not meant to be your "Debby Downer" or to scare you, but rather to prepare you and let you know that stuff happens in life, that you are not alone, and that you can and will get through life's tough, sad, and yucky times.

People will be mean and can make you feel awful.

Ever heard someone say, "She is fat/ugly/a loser?" Or, have you had someone tell you, "No I can't go anywhere with you tonight, I'm sick," and then you see their Instagram photos from a party that they went to without you?

 People will cheat, steal, or lie to your face.

As long as it gets them what they want, people can behave badly in ways you would never expect.

 You will get left out.

On purpose.

 You will get sick.

Sometimes this will happen at the worst possible time (biggest game of the year, holidays, school dance).

 Loved ones get sick or die.

Sickness and death are a terribly sad part of life, but a reality. You definitely need help to get through this, so please seek it out from a TruBlue or a professional.

 Life isn't fair.

Once in a while cheaters win because they didn't get caught (this time). Usually Karma comes back around to bite the liars and cheats at another time.

❌ *You don't always get what you want.*

Things happen when they are supposed to and not always on your clock. Patience is a virtue.

❌ *People will let you down and leave you hanging.*

"Sorry, I went to Kelsy's party instead of yours. I thought I told you."

❌ *You will get beaten to the punch.*

If you don't raise your hand, step out, and say what you want to say, someone else will seize the opportunity first.

❌ **No one else is going to take care of you but you.**

Okay, your parents and TruBlues help, but it's up to you to run your own race, to be the best you can be to yourself.

❌ **If you snooze, you lose.**

Don't wait to be good. Others are always waiting in the wings to take your spot on the team, at work, or at the college of your choice, which happens to also be theirs. So be amazing in all you do. Characteristics like laziness, lack of effort, or procrastination won't help you in life.

❌ *You might make choices based on bad influences.*

You can never take those decisions back. If you make choices based on your Total Package Girl goals, you never have to say, "I knew better, but I did it anyway." Make choices for *your* solid reasons, not someone else's.

The right and smart path isn't always the easy path.

Staying home from the party and studying for the SATs will prove to be the right choice when you get a high score and get into your number-one college choice. Be comfortable doing the right thing.

 Sometimes the other girl will win and you will lose.

You can prepare till the cows come home for the top seat, the job promotion, the competition, but the interviewer may choose someone who you perceive to be less talented than you—or who, perhaps, has better chemistry with or perceived value to the interviewer. The student body at school may vote for someone else for the student council position. It's not the end of the world. You win some in life and you lose some. Stay centered, learn from the experience, and move on. Yes, it hurts, but don't let it keep you from trying again.

 There is almost always someone more skilled than you.

Competition can be steep, and others really really want to reach their dreams just like you do. Not always, but at some point in your life, you will get beat fair and square by someone who's just better than you. Be an honorable loser. If you're highly competitive, this is tough, and you'll have to learn how to lose with grace and style. If you don't get the job or the spot on the dance team, take the high road and be gracious even in defeat. The person who was hired instead of you may repeatedly show up for work late and then get fired, or someone on the dance team may get injured. Guess who is next in line? You! All the more reason to stay positive, appreciative, and hardworking.

⊗ *Hanging out with bad-reputation people will give you the same reputation.*

"Guilt by association" means people judge you (yes, people do judge) by who you hang out with. The driver of the car—the accomplice—goes to jail along with the robber of the ATM. Being in a risky situation, illegal or questionable, will gain you the wrong kind of reputation. Your parents may let you off the hook sometimes, but a police officer won't believe excuses. There are no second chances with the law. Choose your hangout friends and actions wisely.

⊗ *Fun is everywhere if you look for it. So is trouble.*

Don't go looking for trouble. Laugh your head off with good friends and clean fun. Trouble leads you down a completely different path.

⊗ *You will make mistakes.*

Yep, you're gonna make 'em, because no one is perfect. Not the cover girl, supermodel, your favorite celebrity, or the author of this book. Also not perfect are the Total Package Girl, the mean girl, your parents, your teachers, your role models. Everyone makes mistakes.

An absolute reality of being human is that you are going to make mistakes and do dumb things, even though you are trying your best not to. Stuff just happens. We are all human. Doing things with the right idea, intention, or direction will help you through. Accept and go easier on yourself and others when mistakes happen.

⊠ *Some people want to relive your mistakes.*

Believe it or not, some people never want you to forget the mistakes you've made. They choose to keep reminding you. The mistake could have been years ago, but they will keep bringing it up, perhaps as a way to manipulate or keep you down. When that happens, it's time to nip it in the bud by directly telling them, "Leave it alone, stop bringing up the past. I've moved on and I hope you can too." And you may want to move on from that type of person as well.

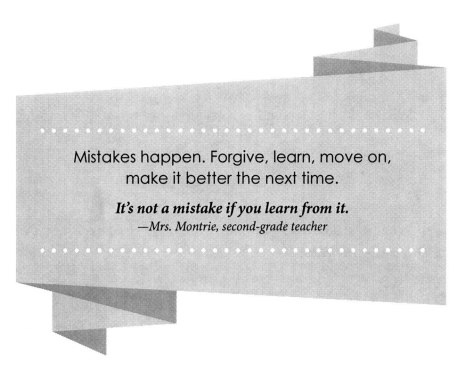

Mistakes happen. Forgive, learn, move on,
make it better the next time.

It's not a mistake if you learn from it.
—Mrs. Montrie, second-grade teacher

TOTAL PACKAGE GIRL ACTIVITY:
My Checkpoint for Mistakes

What big mistakes have I made in life?

☐ _____

☐ _____

What can I learn from those mistakes?

_____

_____

What is the best lesson I've learned from a mistake I've made?

_____

_____

What mistakes have I avoided by making good decisions and trusting my GPS?

_____

What mistakes am I still holding on to that I need to erase so I can move on? *(Hint: Let them go!)*

☐ _____

☐ _____

Surprise slippery slopes will test you.

Sometimes mistakes happen when a situation pops up out of nowhere and you need to make a split-second decision. Like when you're supposed to be home at a certain time and you impulsively get a ride with an upperclassman who decides to go through the drive-through for burgers and then take a joyride and throw Halloween pumpkins around the neighborhood. Not only are you going to be home late, but you also are now in a car with someone who is doing bad things, and you are stuck in an unplanned heap of trouble. You made the mistake of going along and perhaps not asking your parents in the first place and then got stuck on a slippery slope.

Once you get on a slippery slope, use your exit strategy to get out of that situation ASAP. What steps will you take to remove yourself at that moment in time? In the car-ride example, consider your options:

* *You could ask the driver to take you home right then.*

* *You could text your parents if you have a phone and have them meet you somewhere.*

* *You could do nothing and hope you come out of the situation safely and without legal consequences.*

What would your exit strategy be in a situation like that?

 You can't change the past, so carry on.

When you make a mistake, whatever it is—you said something you didn't mean to say, you acted outside of your true personality, you posted something embarrassing—realize you can't go backward and change it. It's done. Assess what you did and why you did it. Learn from it. Be patient and don't beat yourself up over it (even though it can be tough not to).

Ask yourself: Could this have been prevented? How can I never let this happen again? Where did I go wrong and stop following my GPS? Do I need to apologize to someone? What actions can make the situation better? Then forgive yourself. Say "I forgive me" out loud if you have to. Learn from the experience by trying not to repeat the same mistake, and then let go of it.

Insight: The letting-go part is super-hard to do, but necessary for you to get back to your true Total Package Girl path. Don't keep talking about it, judging it, or giving it energy. Leave it in your past. Lesson learned. Forgive yourself. Carry on.

❎ *Nothing lasts forever.*

Well, okay, a few things in life are forever. But so often it seems that just when everything's comfortable, something comes along and shakes it up a bit. Ever notice that? There is an expression: "People come into your world for a reason, a season, or a lifetime." You will have people in your life for a certain chapter—say, an elementary school mean girl. She was there to teach you something, perhaps about standing up for yourself or another person, or how to not back down. Then perhaps she moved away. She was there for a reason and a season.

Same thing is true when it comes to your life direction. You might travel down a certain smooth path for a year. Then you realize it wasn't the right path for you, but you wouldn't have known that until you traveled it. An example is if you took a job that wasn't a good match for you. At first you were excited about it, but you soon realized you weren't good at it, and you didn't enjoy it. It was clear that it was time to move on—or perhaps you even got fired from the job. You learned a valuable lesson about yourself, what job you may or may not be good at, and what skills you may or may not possess.

The same might be true in a relationship with a person who isn't a good match personality-wise. Perhaps you like someone who turns out to be conniving, a risk-taker, or a mean person. You may not know if it's a right or wrong match for you until you are already in the relationship. If this happens to you, and you discover the match feels wrong, no need to panic. Remember, it isn't forever. Develop your exit strategy for that relationship and tell the person it's not right. Here, the end is a good thing. Close that door. A new one will be waiting.

Endings mean beginnings.
When something ends, look ahead and see
life's new doors waiting to be opened by you.
#TotalPackageGirlDreams

Insight: When something ends, something else begins. If you exit a bad relationship, learn a lesson from it and know that there is a new, better one waiting around the corner. You may be sad, but be excited, too, for the new possibilities. Trust your inner Total Package Girl to know when it's time to walk away or take a new path. *Never sacrifice personal health or safety to stay in an unhealthy situation.* Once you exit, look ahead to the future and leave the negative door behind you closed.

 You won't always know what to do.

Sometimes in life, you really and truly will have no idea what to do in a situation, and you won't want to make a mistake. Here are some steps to consider when you are unsure of what to do:

 Do nothing.

It's perfectly fine to stop, wait for some time to pass before making a decision. Rushing into something or doing something in the spur of the moment isn't always a good thing and actually can make your confusion worse.

 Talk to a TruBlue.

 *Do the **right** thing, not necessarily the **popular** thing.*

This rule will lead you back to your Total Package Girl path. When everyone goes out to eat on a Saturday night after the basketball game, that, in theory, is a fine, right choice. However, when your peers tell their parents they are going out to eat but instead go to a party with alcohol, the right thing here is not the popular thing. The right thing here might mean going home and pulling out a good book.

Know there may be a difference between right and popular, so use your discernment skills (see Secret Weapon #2). In that same group after the basketball game, maybe someone wants you to take a drink of alcohol, but you don't want to. You need to do the right thing—which, in this case, is listening to your inner Total Package Girl and leave using your exit strategy. Make (or fake) an incoming phone call or text; text a parent for help; or leave the room. Do not take a drink. A police officer may show up and see you drinking, or a person may take a picture of you. The right thing is to exit ASAP.

 Pray for the right answer to come.

Clarity will appear. It always does. It may not be instant. Be patient.

 Lay out the facts that are in plain sight.

If you need to make a quick decision, make it based on all the facts you have at that time. Discern trouble from fun. Go home with your parents or a TruBlue if that's what you decide is the right thing. Trust the facts that appear right in front of you. The answer is usually there all along (like Dorothy).

Insight: Remember Secret Weapon #1 to be your own detective? Look around the group you are in after that basketball game. Assess who's there and the actions they are taking. Are some known for getting into trouble? Are they really nice kids who are fun yet don't find themselves in trouble? Think of future ramifications as they relate to your reputation, health, treatment of others, and the law.

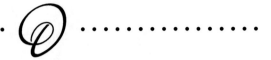

That Girl: A Story

That Girl earned her master's degree and was interviewing for career jobs. Following a big interview, she didn't know if she should take the job she was being offered because something didn't feel right with the potential boss she was interviewing with. He made inappropriate comments about her legs and made her feel uncomfortable with his eye contact. She waited a couple of days before declining the job that was offered to her even though it would have been amazing for her resume.

She later learned that the boss was involved in a sexual-harassment scandal with other young women in the office. To herself, she said, "I knew it!"

That Girl was right. She listened to her inner voice. She dodged a bullet. Eventually, she got a job with a respectful boss who treated her very well. The facts were in plain sight in front of her, and thankfully she was able to use them to discern trouble from truth. She gained more confidence in her decision-making skills.

 Shut down outside noise.

When you don't know what to do but voices are telling you, "Come on, let's go," or "You don't have to ask your parents," learn to quiet the loud voices of others and listen for your Total Package Girl voice of reason to kick in. When pressure mounts, often you already know the answer, but outside noise is interfering. Ever have a hard time connecting to Wi-Fi because you have so many wireless networks and no password? Once you match the right password with the right network, access is immediate. Just like the right Wi-Fi connection and password, when you connect with your inner girl voice by shutting down outside noise, voilà!—the answer will be there.

 Use your exit strategy.

You may need to confront a person face to face, walk away, call a parent to come and get you, avoid a future situation where an unhealthy person is, and send a clear message to the person that this is no longer healthy for you and you are choosing to not hang around anymore. Move on. Exit the situation.

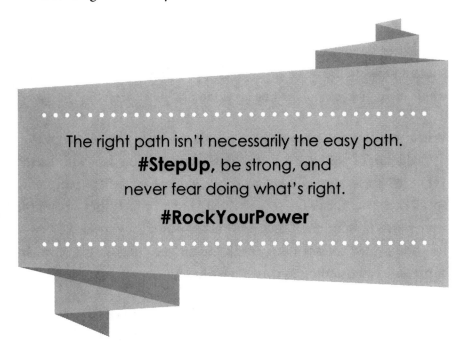

The right path isn't necessarily the easy path. **#StepUp,** be strong, and never fear doing what's right. **#RockYourPower**

Learn (v.)

To discover, become aware, gain knowledge.

Learn and grow from every absolute reality in your life.

[X] **People will try to shut you down.**

The world deserves to hear you. You are too amazing to be a bystander in your own life, especially when it comes to your feelings. Ever sit back in the classroom and when the teacher asks a question, you know the answer but don't raise your hand or respond? Then, when another student answers the question correctly, you think, *I knew that! Wish I would have spoken up.* Don't be afraid to use your own voice.

When you do speak up, ever have people talk over you, interrupt you, or make fun of you in front of others? How did you deal with them? While it's their human right to speak, do not let others repeatedly speak over you, speak for you, or quiet your words. If they do, repeat your words or opinion. If they don't listen—or if they speak for you—feel free to say, "Please don't speak for me" or "Excuse me, I would appreciate you listening to what I have to say."

True, it can be downright scary to speak up in front of a large group of people and say what you feel, because you don't know how others will respond. Will they make fun of you, laugh, argue? Truth is, **#jbu**—and guess what? You may very well spark a great conversation with your valuable comments. Express your thoughts with **#confidence.**

If others do laugh at you, let them laugh. You cannot control their actions, only your own. Trust that your words are intelligent, justified, and on point, and don't let others repeatedly shut you down. You deserve to have your voice heard.

Stop listening to everyone else's voice
so you can hear your own.
Rock your secret weapons and **#jbu**.

#TotalPackageGirl

TOTAL PACKAGE GIRL TOOL:
Your Voice Has Power

 What you have to say is relevant and important. Never forget that.

 Your voice is beautiful, so speak up, speak out, use it to compliment another, to express your opinions and thoughts, to sing, to teach others, to laugh out loud.

 When you express how you feel, things get exciting: you start conversations, people get to know the real you better, you form a connection with others, you attract people who have similar values, you explore your differences, and you find people who respect and like you for who you are.

 You gain respect and show leadership when you use your voice. That puts you in the driver's seat, not the backseat, when it comes to taking charge and leading situations in your life.

 Your relationships may improve when you articulate your feelings—with your parents, teachers, peers. Doors may open with people you never even knew you had so much in common with.

You may spark a new project, ignite change, and make someone else think differently by speaking up and expressing your thoughts and opinions. Believe in the power of you.

 Your voice isn't wrong. It's a reflection of your opinions and feelings. Let it roar.

 Your inner voice is strong and will tell you what to do.

 You are responsible for you.

You've almost always had a safety net, right? When you were younger and you didn't do your best work in school, teachers let you make test corrections for full credit. If you made a mistake, your parents helped you correct it. As you got older, not many teachers offered test corrections, saying, "You get what you get on a test." It's a bit of a harsh reality if you've always had someone taking care of you, protecting you, giving you second chances, and picking you up as soon as you fell.

Same holds true in the real world as you get older. You now must accept consequences for your choices, good or bad. It's absolute reality. If and when you participate in risky behavior, you can no longer blame others because *you* made the choice. It's tough love, but you are responsible for you. You may have to take a *C* rather than an *A* if you truly didn't bother to study for the exam. Own it.

> *Lead* by making the responsible choices
> that are too scary for others to make.
> **#StepUp #TotalPackageGirl**

⊠ Life choices get confusing.

Every day, you are faced with choices. Making them involves choosing safe vs. risky, fun vs. boring, good vs. evil, smart vs. stupid. Specific choices might include studying vs. playing games on your phone, going to a party vs. staying home, trying out for the team or not, staying in the relationship you are in or not.

SAFE ? STUPID ? EVIL
FUN ? GOOD
RISKY ? SMART ? BORING

Confusing, right? That's a lot of choices coming at you, and it's true, you cannot ignore these choices because they don't go away. Thus, sorting through the confusion and making solid decisions is key.

To some girls, making risky choices may seem fun, cool, and exciting. It may even appear that the so-called popular kids at school are using drugs and/or drinking. But don't be fooled. That kind of popularity quickly evaporates when they get kicked off the sports team, are ineligible, or don't get into college. For those who take high risks, there is no reward at the end of the rainbow. Stay true to your Total Package Girl Secret Weapons. They are there to help you make smart, savvy choices so you can have an amazing future and reach your dreams.

When you are facing a confusing decision, remember this: You can't take back or erase the results of bad choices as if they never happened. Choose good over evil, right over wrong, safe over risky when you feel confused. In life, you may face serious issues with permanent consequences like drug addiction, teen pregnancy, school ejection, or a criminal record. No do-overs. Even if you apologize, feel regret, and feel awful, you cannot turn back time. Like the digital footprints you've made in social media, these, too, are the footprints of your life. When things get confusing, do your best to make smart, savvy choices the first time to avoid permanent damage. Talk these confusing issues through with a TruBlue—that always helps.

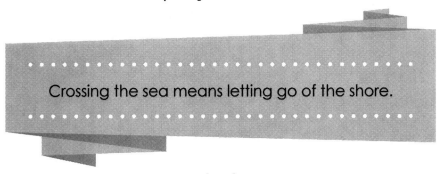

Crossing the sea means letting go of the shore.

TOTAL PACKAGE GIRL ACTION:
Think Ahead

You are about to ride along in a car with a co-ed group of buddies on a weekend night. They decide to get risky and rob the carryout just to be crazy. You want no part of it, but they say, "Jump in." Before you know it, you are a passenger in the car headed toward the carryout. It all happens so fast. The alarm sounds. The police show up. Your friends get arrested and so do you. You are now going to trial for being an accomplice in an attempted robbery, likely doing jail time.

What could you have done differently to change the outcome of this situation?

How can you think ahead and help yourself avoid risky situations in the future?

⊠ For every action, there's a reaction.

All you science buffs know just what we're talking about here. Every action has a reaction—like when you were little, if you reached up and touched the hot stove, you suffered the immediate consequence of burned fingers. Even though you were told not to, you did it anyway and learned the hard way not to ever do that again. When those blisters and burn marks appeared on your fingers from the stove, you were reminded of your painful lesson. For your action there was a reaction: a consequence in this case. Rewards and/or consequences come back to you, just like a boomerang.

As you got a little older, you learned not to run onto the busy street. You may have learned that lesson by a car blaring its horn when it almost hit you as you ran onto the street to chase your soccer ball. These learned behaviors were high-risk with no reward, and you learned to avoid the risks. Thank goodness we all live and learn from our experiences.

As you get older, risks continue to happen, but the stakes are different and can be higher. No longer is it your soccer ball rolling onto the road and you running in front of a car not knowing any better. No longer is it touching a hot stove. You've grown from those experiences. Now, a risky path may include scarier things like drugs, unsafe relationships, jail time. In today's world, things like random drug testing, cell-phone photos being taken and posted, and hidden cameras everywhere make it easier to get caught doing risky things. Not to mention your personal safety—your life—may be at stake if you get involved in risky behavior.

Boomerang risks—with consequences and no do-overs—include:

* *Taking (or being with someone who possesses or is taking) drugs like: marijuana, heroin, cocaine, prescription medications, certain cigarettes, hallucinogens, powder alcohol*

* *Drinking alcohol, drunk driving, or getting in the car with someone who is drinking, buzzed, or drunk*

* *Playing danger games: cinnamon challenge, vodka gummy bears, cough-medicine concoctions—all will land you in a heap of trouble*

* *Buying alcohol as a minor*

* *Possessing a fake ID*

* *Having unhealthy social media/online encounters*

* *Lying to authority*

* *Cheating*

* *Stealing*

* *Using nicotine (e.g., smokeless tobacco, clove cigarettes, pipes)*

* *Sexting/sexual promiscuity*

* *Being an accomplice to any illegal act*

* *Many other activities not listed*

CAUTIONARY NOTE!

No matter how cool or popular someone is thought to be, if he or she participates in high-risk behavior, there will be consequences, such as getting kicked off the team, being ineligible for future scholarships, getting arrested, developing a sexually transmitted disease, not getting letters of recommendation for college, not getting hired for a job, and the list goes on.

If you find yourself being tempted to participate in any of these activities or if you cannot escape someone who is harassing you into participating in any of the above, seek the help of a TruBlue, a professional, a trusted administrator at your school—ASAP.

 Peer pressure is everywhere.

Personal strength, courage, and willpower beat out peer pressure every time. You know that peer pressure and temptation are absolute realities in life. These come in all shapes and sizes, often when you least expect them. Peers who pressure may be convincing, subtle, and nice as pie; or they may be more obvious, high-pressure salespeople, chronic partiers, liars, cheaters, and notorious bad girls or guys. Either way, keep your antennae up for these types. They lurk.

Operation: PARENT says 51 percent of teen girls cite pressure from guys as a reason to send explicit messages via their cell phones. Be in the other 49 percent.

TOTAL PACKAGE GIRL ACTIVITY:
Temptations I've Already Avoided

Life has chapter after chapter: childhood, elementary school, junior high, high school, college/grad school, career, marriage, family, and so on. Many people have already come into your life and temptation has already presented itself.

How have I already resisted temptation in my life?

What future risks and negative temptations do I foresee in my future? How will I handle them?

Proactivity Rocks!

In absolute-reality moments, you can be proactive or reactive.

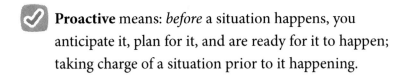 **Proactive** means: *before* a situation happens, you anticipate it, plan for it, and are ready for it to happen; taking charge of a situation prior to it happening.

Reactive means: *after* a situation has already occurred, you then respond to the potential consequences of it.

Imagine someone asks you to post an inappropriate selfie or a cyberbullying comment on Instagram. You are about to do it. Stop and think *proactively*:

* *What could happen to me if I were to do this?*

* *What do I have to lose or gain from this action?*

* *How would the other person feel about this negative, cyberbullying post?*

* *How would I feel about my inappropriate selfie?*

* *How will this decision affect me and my family now and in the future?*

* *Who could potentially see it?*

* *If I do this, would I feel comfortable telling my teachers, my parents, and the whole school what I posted?*

* *Would I be comfortable if my teacher showed this in class?*

* *Would I be proud of myself or feel bad the next day?*

After thinking about all of these things, you likely will choose not to cyberbully or post inappropriately.

Now imagine a situation where you went ahead and impulsively posted the inappropriate or mean post—that is, you were reactive because you didn't think through the consequences, and you frankly didn't care about them at that moment in time. You just quickly wanted to post. Now, at this point, you can only react to what others have to say about it. If and when they react with criticism or harsh comments, you will suffer consequences because you did not think your action through ahead of time. You were reactive. Now you regret what you did, but it's too late. The horse is out of the barn, as they say. How do you feel now?

The bigger question to ask yourself proactively is: Why do I even want to take a negative action, such as posting this picture or cyberbullying someone? Is someone telling me to do it? Who is this person I'm letting control me? Am I following someone else who did the same thing because I want to be like that person or fit in? Why am I wanting to make fun of another person on social media? Knowing *why* you want to do something is important because it may help you resist the urge to do it. Remember how to discern right from wrong, and use self-discipline to stop yourself proactively.

It takes courage and self-discipline to stop a negative post. It takes *no* courage to be a cyberbully.
#RockYourPower #StopMeanWords

You may not realize it, but life has already presented you with proactive and reactive challenges—maybe on a sports team, when you had to dig down deep, work your tail off proactively in the pre-season, and perform your best at the state championships, or maybe at school when someone asked you to cheat and you knew it was wrong so you refused. Those were proactive. You see, you've already been tested and have used your Total Package Girl Secret Weapons to pass with flying colors.

On the opposite end of the spectrum, if you didn't study much for the chapter test thinking you had an "A" wrapped up for the semester but then got a bad grade, you reactively talked with the instructor to see if you could re-take the test because you lost your "A." The answer was no. Proactivity is your friend.

The Adrenaline Rush

Ever feel it? You're getting ready to plummet down the huge hill on the latest roller coaster for the first time. Or you are ready to challenge yourself on the latest high-ropes course at camp. The adrenaline is rushing big time.

Running with a risky crowd can also be a big adrenaline rush. High-risk adrenaline pumps before or during the risky behavior, like trying drugs or alcohol—and once you start, you might not be able to stop. In this case, the adrenaline is like the devil fooling you into thinking your actions will have some kind of reward.

You will always and forever regret a negative decision that harms your body, your health, or your future dreams. Your actions may be irreversible—making permanent footprints and leaving you alone, hooked, or on a downward spiral. Have the self-discipline to choose "fun and safe" over "risky and tempting," no matter how tempting the adrenaline rush might seem.

●　●

☒ Bullies exist.

Whether it's in the cyber world or in person, you know that bullies exist. If you've ever experienced bullying, you know it's awful. Bullies don't care if they are mean or evil. They lack a moral filter. They are like predators in the animal world, preying on those weaker or kinder or gentler or different than they are or who they perceive cannot stick up for themselves. Their mission of making others feel horrible about themselves somehow makes them feel good.

Remember, you cannot control bullies' words or actions, only your own. What they are saying is meant to be evil and hurtful. They want to get a reaction from you for any number of reasons—it could be because they deep down perceive you as weaker than they are, or they may be jealous of you. Who knows their true motivation? At these trying times, use your Power Shield and know these truths:

❉　*Truth is, bullies are cowards.*

❉　*Truth is, those being bullied are strong and courageous.*

✷ *Truth is, you don't need these types in your life, getting in the way of your dreams.* Their future is not bright. On the Noise Spectrum, they are Noisy and Don't Matter. However, that noise can really make you miserable while it's going on. If you are bullied, remember you have a Power Shield to keep you strong. **#RightNow**, use it to stand up for yourself (literally, too—with good posture and eye contact when necessary) and be the bravest, strongest person you've ever been. Never let bullies get into your mind or spirit. Keep them out and find your positives—your Total Package Girl TruBlues, your **#MeMantras**, your secret weapons, and your Power Shield. Don't be afraid to use them.

Bullying is not to be taken lightly or to be kept to yourself. Don't endure the hurt or negative behavior alone. Use the following tool as a guide but also seek help from a TruBlue, a trusted authority and/or professional if this is happening to you. Report it when you see it happening to another as well. No one should ever have to go through bullying alone.

For evil to triumph less, it follows that good people need to do something—like exposing wickedness when they are confronted with it.
—M.H. Levinson

TOTAL PACKAGE GIRL TOOL:
Bully Action Plan

 Stay calm. Take slow, deep breaths. (Think Power Shield.) Walk away.

 Save evidence. Don't erase the bully's texts, e-mails, posts, or journal entries you've written to document the situation.

 Remember that bullies are not worth your time. Try not to outwardly react to them. This gives them and their actions energy, which you do not want to do.

 Stay super-close to your TruBlues, who are vital **#RightNow**. Don't close them out; get hugs from them and talk with them about what is happening. Share your feelings with a TruBlue who will help you through this difficult time that you didn't create. Do not be embarrassed or timid. You are courageous. Bullies are cowardly.

 If you're being bullied on the Web, block the bully and do not talk excessively about the incident to kids at school. The less "noise" about it, the better. Again, you don't want to give these people or their actions any energy or motivation to keep doing it.

 Don't accept anyone you are trying to confide in about the situation telling you that you need to "get a thicker

skin," "toughen up," or "let it go." Those responses are not helpful if you are feeling so terrible that you can't sleep or cannot go to school because the situation is nasty and negative. Don't give up if someone tells you that; find someone else who will listen and help you. **#TruBlue**

 Avoid the bully or the bullying location if and when possible by taking a different route or not responding to cyber comments. Act like the bully is nonexistent. Get a friend or adult to walk with you or sit with you.

 Remember the amazing attributes of you. Know that you are never alone, even though it may feel that way at the time. Someone loves you **#RightNow.**

 Never be afraid to tell authorities or teachers if someone is bullying you. Be relentless in letting authorities know that this person is big trouble.

 If you see someone else being bullied, don't hesitate to stick up for that person and tell the bully to stop. Take action; perhaps start an anti-bullying campaign if it feels like the right thing to do.

 If you ever find yourself acting like a bully, stop immediately and apologize to the victim. Get help if you cannot stop.

Dream blockers kill your vibe.

There may be things in your life that are keeping you from reaching your dreams. These "dream blockers" are absolute realities that may be holding you back from future success, like a wall built up around you or a mountain in front of you that you don't want to climb.

. . . .

Dream Blocker (n.)

Something (real or imagined) that keeps you from reaching your dreams, from being you. It's an obstacle, a hurdle, a wall, or a behavior that is currently holding you back.

*Letting others' negative comments influence you is a **dream blocker** because it keeps you from doing what you love to do by affecting your self-esteem, your beliefs, and the choices you make.*

. . . .

The trick is to identify and then attack dream blockers—the sooner the better. "Nip it in the bud," as they say. A dream blocker goes deeper than a bad habit like biting your nails or tapping your fingers on the desk in class. The dream blocker actually holds you back.

TOTAL PACKAGE GIRL ACTIVITY:
What Are My Dream Blockers?

Check the list of dream blockers below that might be holding you back from being #TheUltimateYouForLife. Write any others on the next page. Remember, no one is perfect, so no judgments. Be honest with yourself and dig deep here. This is a self-awareness activity. After this, you can work to eliminate what's holding you back and blocking your dreams.

My dream blockers are:

☐ Worrying or stressing out

☐ Fear (of:)

☐ Gossiping and mean talk

☐ Envying others/jealousy

☐ Repeatedly making poor relationship choices

☐ Hanging out with negative influences

☐ Acting dramatic or like a victim for attention when I am not one

☐ Negatively talking about myself or not using my voice to **#StandUp**

☐ Possessing low self-esteem; letting others talk negatively to me, not believing in the power of me

>> *More on the next page.*

- [ ] Acting "too cool for school," excessively bragging

- [ ] Being disrespectful, unthankful or ungrateful; taking advantage of others

- [ ] Not taking care of my health

- [ ] Behaving illegally or taking unnecessary or unhealthy risks

List other dream blockers here:

- [ ]
- [ ]
- [ ]

Attacking Dream Blockers

Now that you've identified your dream blocker(s), it's time to stop the stranglehold they have on you.

Some say it takes twenty-one days to establish a new habit and break a bad one. Dream blockers are different than habits, so you can begin **#RightNow** to replace the grip your blockers have on you. How? Here are some Total Package Girl steps to attack and lose a dream blocker:

 Visualize yourself living without the blocker and notice how free you feel. Pay attention to how you feel when you see your new self without it.

✅ *Write a three-step action plan to eliminate the blocker.* Then set reminder notes and/or text alerts to keep you on track and stop the behavior that's keeping your dream blocker alive.

✅ *Surround yourself with positive influences*—people who build you up, not tear you down—to help you lose behaviors or thoughts that keep the blocker hanging around.

List positive influences here:

⭐

⭐

⭐

Write my three-step action plan here:

1️⃣

2️⃣

3️⃣

✅ *Stay away from triggers that pull you back to the dream blocker,* like those who continue gossiping when you are trying to stop, or continue to be mean to you when you are trying to stay away from negative influence.

✓ *Try releasing the dream blocker "cold turkey" (all at once),* while understanding that you've been hanging on to it like a baby hangs on to a security blanket. Be patient with yourself.

✓ *Catch yourself in the act of doing dream blocker actions.* If you are a negative self-talker, when you say degrading comments about yourself, stop immediately and correct your words by saying something positive about yourself right away. You will likely have some failed attempts, but stay with it. The more you use a muscle, the stronger it gets. The same principle applies here. It will get easier.

✓ *Re-visit your Total Package Girl Pact from Part I.*

✓ *Have a no-excuse mentality.*

✓ *Stay disciplined and keep your footsteps moving in a positive, forward direction.* You will be a changed person once you lose your dream blockers.

Re-focus today on
power, energy, fitness, and health.

With the new day comes new strength and new thoughts.
—Eleanor Roosevelt

Insight: We sometimes hang on to dream blockers because we fear letting them go. If your dream blocker is "gossip" and people know you as the one who is the ringleader in the gossip world, when you suddenly stop gossiping about other people, it may mean that the frenemies will stop talking to you. That may be scary or uncomfortable at first, yet your world may very well change for the better quickly thereafter.

If you shut down others' overly dramatic gossip, they may not want to tell you mean things anymore. Is that bad? At first it may seem odd to be free from the gossip dream blocker, but you will quickly begin to notice that the quality of your conversations and the people surrounding you may get a lot deeper, and that gossipy types will find another person to spread rumors with. Let your dream blockers go. Wave good-bye for good.

As Confidence Grows, Dream Blockers Fade

When you hang on to dream blockers, you block your self-confidence and your life dreams, like clouds block sun rays. Don't be afraid to clear away the clouds. They are hovering and keeping you away from the real you. As you let dream blockers go, you will feel more clarity and **#confidence.**

Fear (n.)

A belief that something is potentially dangerous, unsafe, or painful.

Fear can immobilize us and keep us from our true passions and dreams. When conquered, fear is powerless.

❌ You'll experience mental hopscotch.

Based on life's unpredictable realities, you might find yourself having a lot of emotions, even in one twenty-four-hour period, and they can be all over the board. One minute you're mad, one you're excited, then back to upset about something. Feelings can change day to day, hour to hour, even minute to minute. That's pretty normal for this time in life.

Because emotions can be high and low, be patient and nonjudgmental with yourself. Call it "mental hopscotch"—the ups and downs of your emotions. Your Total Package Girl Secret Weapons and tools will help at these times, and so will your ability to check in with your emotions so you can identify and know how to better respond when you feel a certain way.

CAUTIONARY NOTE!

As always, it is advised to seek professional help if you ever feel that you need additional assistance in talking about and taking care of you and your emotions. Be brave.

TOTAL PACKAGE GIRL TOOL:
Emotion Checker

Use the following Total Package Girl Emotion Checker to check in on the emotions you feel at any given time. This tool may help you better understand yourself by offering suggestions that clear the fog away, so you can make a solid decision, understand yourself better, and/or figure out the right thing to do. *Add your own ideas, or a TruBlue's, or a professional's, at the end of each section on the "My Other Ideas" line.*

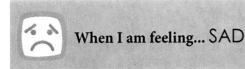

When I am feeling... SAD

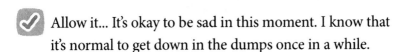

Allow it... It's okay to be sad in this moment. I know that it's normal to get down in the dumps once in a while.

Pray about the sadness and ask for the situation to be healed.

[193]

- ✅ Ask: "Why I am feeling sad? What or who does this involve? Why is it so sad?"

- ✅ Do something to make my heart feel better: Talk to a TruBlue, take a walk, pick a flower and notice its beauty.

- ✅ **#TPJournalIt** to articulate what's sad and why.

- ✅ Know the sadness cloud isn't here forever. It will dissipate and sun rays will shine on me again.

- ✅ My other ideas:

When I am feeling... LIKE SOMEONE TREATED ME UNFAIRLY

- ✅ Let her/him know that she/he was unfair to me and tell her/him why I feel this way.

- ✅ If the situation has already passed but I'm still upset, I get to decide whether I need to say something at all or if I should move on.

- ✅ Remember that somebody loves me **#RightNow**, and that I am awesome and beautiful inside and out.

- ✅ Remember what my intentions were and that I acted in

the right way and that this might be "on them" not on me.

- ✅ Think of how I can keep this from happening again and be stronger the next time.

- ✅ As I begin to let it go, know that others love me for me, so I will focus on those who treat me fairly and with respect. **#TruBlue**

- ✅ **#TPJournalIt** to discover why this feels unfair.

- ✅ My other ideas: _____

 When I am feeling... HAPPY

- ✅ Embrace and celebrate this amazing feeling. **#RightNow**

- ✅ Ask: "Why do I feel happy? What or who is it that made me feel this way?" I will remember the things in life that make me feel this happy and keep doing them.

- ✅ I will ride the happy wave—do a happy dance, go outside and run, go to the mall, listen to my favorite music, start a new hobby, call someone I haven't talked to in a long time, pick wildflowers.

- ✅ **#TPJournalIt.**

✅ Remember to share the happy times with those I love or by myself.

✅ Pray by saying thank you for this wonderful moment.

✅ My other ideas: _____

 When I am feeling... EMBARRASSED

✅ There will be times when I wake in the morning after something embarrassing happened and say, "Please tell me that was just a dream." But if it really happened, ask, "Why am I so embarrassed?"

✅ Ask: "Who saw me do this and was it legitimately embarrassing or am I making up some drama?" Was the "embarrassment" important in the overall scheme of life?

✅ Does the situation require an apology? How so?

✅ Say, "I forgive myself because we all make mistakes and do silly things." Laugh it off, learn from it and move on. It's over.

✅ Know that I may likely be the only one to remember this later, so take the imaginary eraser and erase it.

✓ #TPJournalIt.

✓ My other ideas: _____

 When I am feeling... GUILTY ABOUT SOMETHING I DID

✓ Ask: "Why did I do that?" and "How can I make this right?"

✓ Understand my actions. Then forgive myself. Take steps to move forward knowing that I will do better the next time and not have a repeat performance.

✓ Pray for a fresh start or for forgiveness, and have the courage to jump back on my Total Package Girl path.

✓ Choose future actions with my GPS aimed at positive energy, brightness, and optimism.

✓ Follow my positive inner girl thoughts and apologize if needed to the person to whom I did wrong.

✓ #TPJournalIt.

✓ Discuss my action with a TruBlue.

✓ My other ideas: _____

When I am feeling... ALONE

☑ What's making me feel alone **#RightNow**? Another person? A circumstance that happened? Did I step out of my comfort zone and experience something for the first time and learn a valuable lesson? Has a personal status changed, such as a relationship, location, job, school, etc.?

☑ Remind myself: no worries. Everything will be all right.

☑ Remember that I don't have to depend on someone else for my happiness. I can be resourceful and **#jbu**, alone in my thoughts—and that's okay.

☑ Ask: "Am I tired or sleep deprived?" (That can make anyone feel glum at times.)

☑ Remember, quiet time can be very healthy, so I need to get comfortable with being alone in my thoughts to discover my deeper feelings. This helps me grow, listen to my inner girl, and figure out life.

☑ Take this alone feeling and self-reflect on my positive attributes, talents, and loves.

☑ Remember that something and someone new and exciting are around the corner.

✓ Know that someone loves me and cares for me **#RightNow**, even though I feel alone at this moment.

✓ Call a TruBlue.

✓ **#TPJournalIt**.

✓ My other ideas: ....

Insight: Sometimes you might feel alone if, say, you've chosen to stay home from a party or from something you felt uncomfortable doing. It's okay to spend time alone, even though at first it feels strange or lonely. Especially when you make such a smart decision, give yourself some props for stepping up and being brave by not entering a potentially risky situation.

Or, you might feel alone because you weren't invited to something that others were. In life, everybody isn't friends with everybody; unfortunately, this stuff happens and it hurts. This might be a great time to think about some new friendships and new possibilities that are better for you and are opening up to you. If you feel lonely much of the time, be brave and ask for professional help.

When I am feeling... CONFUSED or LOST

✓ Sort out my thoughts and **#TPJournalIt**. The goal is to get to the heart of my feelings. Write down each confusing thought one at a time. Write down details of each thought until the confusion gets clearer.

✓ Ask: "What is the issue I'm confused about? Is the confusion about a person? School? Life direction? A situation that isn't sitting right with me?"

✓ Ask: "Am I getting enough sleep? Am I getting over an illness?"

✓ Discuss my feelings of confusion with a TruBlue to begin sorting them out verbally.

✓ Ask: "Is there a resource I can turn to?" Consider discussing my situation in the Total Package Lifestyle app chat room.

✓ Assess the next steps on my Total Package Girl path. Am I starting a new chapter in my life and do I need to reset my goals and dreams?

✓ What do I want to focus on **#RightNow** in my life? What are my current loves and interests?

✓ Who do I want to hang around with who is fun, healthy, positive?

✓ Once I sort through this more, plan activities that I like to do normally that align with my Total Package Girl path, like a fun trip to the mall, park, or museum.

✓ My other ideas: _____

 When I am feeling... BORED

✓ Ask: "Why am I bored? Do I have enough fun things to do and some fulfilling, healthy hobbies?"

✓ Consider my healthy options: I could take a nap; read a good book or magazine; start a new hobby; daydream; do a puzzle or game; call a relative I haven't talked with in a long time; exercise; play with my pet; research a new brain game; go outside and walk in nature.

✓ I will do something healthy and positive, nothing negative.

✓ **#TPJournalIt** and get creative.

✓ My other ideas: _____

When I am feeling... ANGRY

✅ Ask: "Why am I feeling angry and who am I angry at? Am I angry at someone else or at myself for something I did or didn't do and wish I would have?"

✅ How will I make the situation feel better and lessen my anger? Can I talk to the person who was involved (sooner rather than later) or a trusted adult?

✅ Can I take action myself to make the feelings less raw and more positive?

✅ What healthy, positive thing can I do to release some of this anger? Can I go punch my pillow, take a run, talk to a TruBlue, lift weights, go for a bike ride?

✅ #TPJournalIt.

✅ My other ideas:

CAUTIONARY NOTE!

If the anger has gone on for an extended period of time or if it feels deeper than you can address alone, seek professional help as needed. Be brave.

When I am feeling... SCARED OR NERVOUS

✅ Ask: "What is making me feel scared? An upcoming event? A past situation involving mean behavior? A person? Something else?"

✅ Is my safety affected or are people being harmful or hurtful to me?

✅ Am I feeling insecure so I'm imagining or perhaps creating things to worry about (what-if thinking)? **#TPJournalIt** with action steps to make me feel less scared.

✅ Talk with and get a hug from a TruBlue to calm my nerves.

✅ Close my eyes and take slow, deep breaths. Visualize working through my fear.

✅ Identify actions that will make me feel better: Get more information on something so I am no longer afraid; read an inspiring verse or story; schedule an upcoming fun activity.

✅ Take action in the direction of my fear. If I'm afraid of my role in the upcoming play ... run toward my fear by practicing so my fear turns to confidence.

✅ My other ideas:

Insight: Why Girls Worry

Different ages and chapters in life may bring different worries. Part of the reason girls worry is because they may be unprepared for an upcoming situation—not knowing what's going to be on the test, what's going to happen at Homecoming. Another reason is because they've developed a habit of worrying, that "what-if" thinking: What if he doesn't like me? What if she won't talk to me? What if the sky fell?

Girls also worry about making the wrong choice in confusing times and what consequences this will have. No one can predict the future, and many of us would like a crystal ball to know exactly what's going to happen in life: Where will I go to college? Who will I marry? Will I have children, and if so, how many? What will my career be?

Rather than fear the unknown, trust that your future is bright. Make savvy, smart choices now to lessen your worry, and surround yourself with TruBlues. Set dreams and goals for yourself and prepare for future situations. These all lead to your Total Package Girl path of confidence, not worry. #TPJournalIt

When I am feeling... UNSURE IN TIMES OF CHANGE

Change is going to happen. New circumstances may occur at school or home; relationships may change, or friends I thought were loyal may let me down or leave me feeling unsure of myself. At times like these, I will:

- ✓ Pray for clarity and peace. Have faith and trust that my path will be clearer soon. My confidence will return and a new door is waiting for me to open it.

- ✓ Remember that change is a part of life and that this uneasy feeling may not be a bad thing. I may just be anticipating something good and exciting that's coming in my future.

- ✓ Get excited about new friends I will make and new dreams I will set.

- ✓ Hold on to what I know is sure: my TruBlues, my talents, my loves, my spirit. These will help me stay grounded.

- ✓ Spend minimal time with unhealthy people who make me feel bad or keep me from being me. Be super-brave and learn to walk away from a mean girl or bad situation. It's much healthier for me in the long run.

- ✓ Get creative and **#TPJournalIt**.

- ✓ My other ideas: ....

TOTAL PACKAGE GIRL ACTIVITY:
Why I Worry

Change is an absolute reality that is going to happen in my life, and I don't need to be scared about it. When one door closes, another one opens, so I'm going to embrace and anticipate all of the exciting new things that will happen in my life rather than worry about them.

What are the main things I worry about and why?

☐

☐

☐

What exciting people and experiences can I anticipate to replace my "worrying" thoughts?

TOTAL PACKAGE GIRL ACTIVITY:
My Other Emotions

What other emotions do I sometimes feel that aren't listed in the Total Package Girl Emotion Checker?

☐ _____

☐ _____

☐ _____

Insight: You won't always be clear on where life is headed. Focus on making it fun and exciting and full of learning experiences. When it gets a bit scary or discouraging, know this feeling is temporary and that you are often in the driver's seat and can set your GPS. You are equipped with Total Package Girl Secret Weapons to make smart decisions and reach your dreams. Remember, tomorrow's a new day with fresh choices to be made, new people to meet, and new experiences. Move forward by clarifying or resetting your dreams, or perhaps removing unhealthy people or situations from social media, your circle of hang-out friends, your life. You have the power. Enjoy the ride, **#RightNow**.

PART IV

Be the
Total Package Girl
For Life

Your Total Package Girl Master Plan

As a Total Package Girl, you need a Master Plan that covers:

1 Your Body   **2** Your Brain   **3** Your Spirit

All three work together as the *total package* of you.

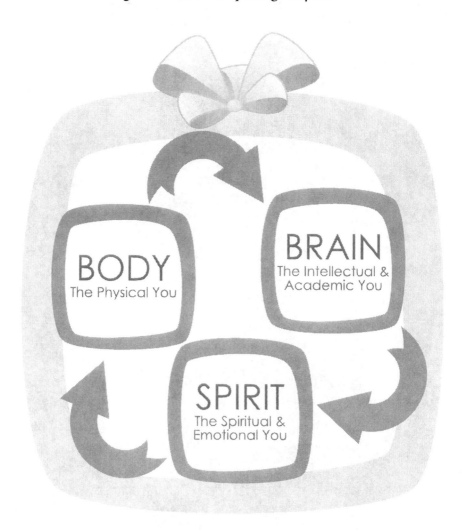

The Total Package Lifestyle

Integrating your Body, Brain, and Spirit Plans into one Master Plan means living the **#TotalPackageLifestyle** inside and out your whole life. That's what a Total Package Girl does. And just like your Total Package Girl Pact says, living the Total Package Lifestyle means:

- *Focusing on a healthy, fit body for life*

- *Trusting and respecting yourself, being positive, and having fun*

- *Doing for others and being kind and loving in spirit*

- *Sharpening your intellect*

- *Trusting yourself to make the best choices you possibly can*

- *Using your secret weapons to focus on positive dreams and goals*

#TotalPackageLifestyle (n.)

A lifetime focus on being fit, healthy, centered, and energetic.

She lives a fun #TotalPackageLifestyle by consistently centering her Body, Brain, and Spirit.

Part One of Your Master Plan Is Your #TotalPackageBody Plan

BODY
BRAIN
SPIRIT

No more listening to what society or the media may tell you your body "should" look like. It's time to step up your own game and know you are going to erase:

✳ *Inaccurate portrayals of the female body*

✳ *The belief that you are not good or pretty enough*

✳ *Negative self-talk*

Erasing these negative thoughts sets you up for reaching your dreams by believing in your own potential, not in what someone else thinks you should look or be like. You begin to celebrate yourself for all of the great things you offer. You set your own agenda.

Insight: In 2007, a popular women's magazine airbrushed a talk-show host's "outie" belly button completely away. Poof, it was gone, replaced by an "innie." Seemingly, the publication didn't want her body to have that belly button so they deleted it—possibly because it was perceived to be an imperfection. This is an excellent reminder of certain mass media's attempts to portray women as "perfect" and not "real."

TOTAL PACKAGE GIRL ACTION:
Positive Self-Talk and
A Healthy Body Image

Today's your day—this **#RightNow** moment—to stop envying or being jealous of airbrushed cover models on magazines and online. No more comparing your body to others'. Your own body is beautiful. Have you told yourself that lately?

It's time to practice positive self-talk and, when it comes to your body, focus on being fit and healthy, not perfect. Certain media enhance images of people, making them thinner, prettier, and more perfect, as we just read. Know and accept this as reality, and you may never feel as insecure about your body again. Focus on the true, amazing you and not on another person's Instagram photo that may have been filtered or retouched.

Now that you've erased the negative never-good-enough mentality, you know that you are amazing exactly the way you were born. When outside voices or media messages get in your head and tell you otherwise, use your Power Shield to remind you that no one can take away the beautiful you. It's in your mind what you choose to believe. **#LoveMeSomeMe**

Here are components to your **#TotalPackageBody** Plan for a fit, energetic, and healthy lifestyle:

⭐ *Nutrition*

⭐ *Workout: exercise, physical strength, flexibility, and more*

⭐ *Sleep*

⭐ *Body beauty and care—skin, hair, teeth, and more*

⭐ *Rockin' body image*

We are each perfectly human,
which makes us all imperfectly perfect.
#jbu and **#LoveYouSomeYou**

Fit girls rock! The goal of your **#TotalPackageBody** Plan is: to be fit, healthy, energetic... and of course, to have fun! Your new lifestyle! Do this for yourself, not for anyone else. The focus is now on staying healthy and fit, and learning positive **#TotalPackageBody** Plan secrets now so they are always a part of your confident Total Package Girl Lifestyle.

 Nutrition

The first **#TotalPackageBody** Plan component is nutrition.

✓ *Think "pure" foods when it comes to fueling your body.* Eat as many natural, earth-growing healthful, nutrition-filled foods you can.*

✓ *Healthy eating starts at the store with smart purchases,* so encourage whoever does the grocery shopping to buy fresh, healthy, non-processed foods whenever possible so you have only healthy foods at your house. Consider organic.

✓ *Do the healthy test before a meal:* Ask yourself, "Am I sure I want to put this food in my body? Does it offer great nutrition and energy for me?" If yes, eat up. Assess each food that goes into your mouth and keep it healthy.

✓ *Minimize (or eliminate) refined sugar*—such as soda pop, candy, and boxed processed foods—from your diet.

✓ *Don't be afraid to eat healthy fats.**

✓ *Drink water.* Add fresh-squeezed lemon juice or a slice of cucumber, if desired.

✓ *When you are feeling the urge to eat, train yourself to use the hunger scale to determine how hungry you really are.* On a scale of 1 to 10 with 10 being the hungriest, assess your body's cues to eat. If you are a seven or above, you truly are hungry and need to eat. If you are a one or a two, you probably are bored or eating out of habit, and not hungry.

- ✅ *Educate yourself* and use reliable, expert resources to give you guidelines on food categories, nutrition, and healthy consumption. Perhaps see a nutritionist or dietitian to get started on a nutrition plan just for you.

- ✅ *Have your very own doctor-approved healthy eating strategy throughout your whole life,* and do not follow others' bad habits. Establish the self-discipline to say no to unhealthy foods, drinks, and habits.

- ✅ *Keep a food journal*—an app or written copy—to get you on track and keep you focused on mindful, smart eating.* When you become mindful or aware of your food intake, you train your brain to say no to unhealthy and yes to healthy.

- ✅ *No obsessing about food.* Make it your Total Package Girl lifestyle to eat healthy. Lose the fad diet mentality of dramatically cutting calories, as this actually hurts your metabolism. Eating nutritionally keeps food in a healthy place in your life. Establish your **#TotalPackageBody** nutrition plan and relax. No need to overthink it. Be patient and reap the benefits of your healthy, fit lifestyle.

* To find out more, go to: **TotalPackageGirl.com/body**.

Workout

A week has 10,080 minutes in it. Setting aside 130 to 150 of those minutes to work out seems small, but it can make a huge impact on your **#TotalPackageBody** and confidence. Check with your doctor first to be sure that the exercise you choose is healthy and appropriate for you. You don't want to lift too-heavy weights because they may damage your joints or muscles, for example. When you do exercise, track your progress by getting the Total Package Girl journal and **#TPJournalIt**.

Here are some tips for the second component of your **#TotalPackageBody** Plan:

✓ *Commit to motion and movement every day.*

✓ *Identify your type of exercise.* What do you love and enjoy doing?

✓ *Where will you exercise?* Does your school or college have a workout facility? Do you have equipment at home? Is there a trainer you can work with to get you on track? Can you go outside or develop a workout room at home using water bottles for weights for example?

✓ *Download our Total Package Lifestyle app on your smartphone or use your Total Package Girl journal.* Identify your ideal healthy weight and proper nutrient intake for a balanced diet.

✓ *Schedule your workout time.* Include the days of the week, the time of day, and the length of your workouts. Put them on your calendar so you don't miss or skip them. Assuming doctor approval and that you've had your annual physical, start with a plan, such as three days a week for approximately thirty-five minutes each day. You may want to set a "total minutes per week" goal. Of that total, talk to your doctor about how much should be cardio, how much should be stretching for flexibility, and how much should be weight-bearing exercise.

 Save money and purchase (or ask for on your birthday) fitness gear, a fitness tracker, weights, or equipment.

Sleep

Love your pillow. Love your bed. Make it comfy and welcoming for you every night. Research shows that up to 40 million Americans may be suffering from sleep disorders and 60 percent have sleep problems three or more nights per week. Know how cruddy you feel when you wake up tired? Do your best to get eight to ten hours of solid sleep every night. This takes self-discipline, but conquer this and you'll like the refreshed you. Total Package Girl sleep routine suggestions are:

 Go to your bedroom at least twenty minutes before you plan to get into bed. This allows enough time to take care of your skin, brush your teeth, and perhaps take a shower. Work and studying all need to be done by the time you head to your bedroom. Don't take them with you.

 If you like, make yourself a cup of warm water (or decaffeinated green tea) with lemon or honey to soothe you.

☑️ *Take a few minutes to lay out your clothes for the following day.*

☑️ *Set your alarm for the exact time you want to rise and then get right out of bed rather than snoozing.*

☑️ *Make sure you have tomorrow's to-do items organized ahead of time so that when you wake up, you are ready to go.* When you are prepared the night before, you sleep better because you aren't worried about the gazillion things you have to do in the morning. You wake up more organized and ready for the day.

☑️ *Read a soothing book or spiritual verse—nothing frightening, disturbing, or graphic.*

☑️ *#TPJournalIt to be grateful for today and for what you have.* (Keep your Total Package Girl journal on your nightstand in case you need to jot down random thoughts.)

☑️ *Turn your lights down to dim.*

☑️ *Then turn the lights out.*

☑️ *Deep breaths.*

☑️ *Prayer.*

☑️ *More deep breaths.*

☑️ *Sleep tight.*

BODY PLAN

Body Beauty and Care

Your body is going to change every year and every decade. At each phase, you'll have special body needs depending on what you are going through at that particular time in your life. Develop healthy routines (including personal hygiene) to take care of your overall physical body.

 Gorgeous Skin

Skin is your body's largest organ. A healthy skin-care plan includes using lotions appropriate for your skin type every day, treating your face and neck with separate creams from the rest of your body. If you have dry skin, especially in winter, use a lotion with extra moisturizer in it. Drink water. Use sunscreen daily, even on cloudy days. Be sure to follow your **#TotalPackageBody** nutrition plan because what you consume definitely affects the quality of your skin. See a dermatologist or esthetician as needed for additional tips tailored to your needs.

 Amazing Smile

Are you taking good care of your teeth? Get regular check-ups with your dentist, floss regularly, and check out the pros and cons of braces if you haven't already had them. Explore teeth whitening if appropriate.

 Healthy Hair

Learn to take care of your hair. Look for quality hair products that match your hair type. Products specifically formulated for wavy, frizzy, straight, and fine hair can assist in keeping your hair clean, healthy, and manageable. Explore fun hair accessories, flat or curling irons, and other ways to give yourself a change of pace, if you so desire.

 Overall Medical Plan

Regular health checks are very important. Make sure you schedule and keep annual exams. The Centers for Disease Control, among other health agencies, recommends monitoring and checking for breast and cervical cancer, skin cancer, and oral health issues. If a vaccination is recommended for you, research it with medical professionals and get it if you (and your parents) feel it is necessary. If you need eye care, a dermatologist, or an orthodontist, make appointments and keep them.

It feels very good to take care of yourself proactively, not reactively. And when you get sick, take care of yourself right away—at the earliest sign of sickness. This may mean getting to your pediatrician or primary care doctor, going to the pharmacy, nourishing with healthy foods, drinking fluids to avoid dehydration, or allowing your body time to simply sleep and recover.

 Rockin' Body Image

There is a startling statistic that Total Package Global would like to wipe off the charts. The National Institute on Media and Family Research says that 40 percent of nine to ten-year-old girls surveyed have tried to lose weight, and by age thirteen, some 53 percent of American girls are unhappy with their bodies. Body image has become a huge issue with girls. Total Package Global believes that each and every girl must begin to love love love who she is and what she looks like.

So, **#RockYourBodyImage #RightNow**. End the misconception of perfectionism, or that others are "better than" you are. End negative self-talk and **#StopMeanWords**. Realize that those who say mean things or cyberbully are cowards. Know that you are more than just physicality.

When you were a little girl, you likely loved who you were. Hopefully this is still the case, but if this feeling of loving yourself has changed, here are some tips to get your rockin' body image back:

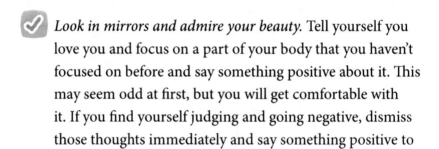 *Look in mirrors and admire your beauty.* Tell yourself you love you and focus on a part of your body that you haven't focused on before and say something positive about it. This may seem odd at first, but you will get comfortable with it. If you find yourself judging and going negative, dismiss those thoughts immediately and say something positive to replace them.

Use #MeMantras (see Secret Weapon #3) and combine them with mirrors. Believe in yourself and your beauty. Love your thighs, your freckles, your hair. Whatever you've been dissing about yourself needs to turn into a positive #**RightNow**. No more negative self-talk. You rock your body like no one else and you offer things to this world that no one else does. Be happy and thrilled that you are *you*. This means don't talk negatively about yourself to others or internally.

✅ *Download our Total Package Lifestyle app* from the App Store™ or on Google Play™ and use our **#MeMantras** to affirm, comfort, encourage, and feel great about yourself.

✅ *In addition to your workout plan, do one healthy #StepUp activity every day* so you feel awesome about your **#TotalPackageBody**. Plan it out ahead of time so you are ready to go. It might be taking a walk in the park, trying a new healthy smoothie recipe, or drinking more water.

✅ *Give yourself kudos for your accomplishments every day.* **#TPJournalIt**. Give thanks for what you have and who you are every single day. **#LoveMeSomeMe**

✅ *Wear an item of clothing that you've been uncomfortable or insecure wearing, such as a bathing suit or a pair of shorts.* Walk with confidence and rock it, holding your head high and smiling that gorgeous smile of yours. Dismiss negative feelings and **#RockYourBodyImage**.

✅ *Avoid envying pictures of celebrities portrayed in the media as having perfect bodies, skin, and hair.* Remind yourself that magazine covers are often airbrushed, with girls' and women's body shapes, skin, or hair altered in some way. Rather, love your natural body and be thankful for its beauty.

Part Two of Your Master Plan Is Your #TotalPackageBrain Plan

Your *Brain Plan* represents that you value your intellectual, smart self, that you choose to make wise choices, and that you want be the sharpest, savviest girl you can be in life. Having a #TotalPackageBrain Plan means you implement the following:

 Big Dreams

Set your big-picture dreams and life goals and where you'd like to be in future years—one, five, ten, and twenty-five years from now. Don't allow yourself to say "I don't know yet" or "I'm not sure." Get specific and have fun as you think about your future plans and **#TPJournalIt**. As you reach your dreams and goals, reset (recalibrate) them so you have new ones to work toward. Keep dreaming. It's important to **#TPJournalIt** so you know where you are **#RightNow** and where your Total Package Girl GPS is set.

 Intellectual Growth

Find and take time to read all genres of books and use your imagination. Sharpen your knowledge in an area you've always been interested in but have yet to explore and then imagine the possibilities. For example, read a biography on a former first lady, a historical fiction book, or a how-to book. Pick a topic you've always wanted to learn about or someone you've wanted to know more about.

Challenge yourself for some step-up learning with online quizzes; download world geography or trivia apps; do Sudoku, crossword puzzles, and IQ teasers; or take on a tricky thousand-piece puzzle to challenge your brain. **#StepUp**

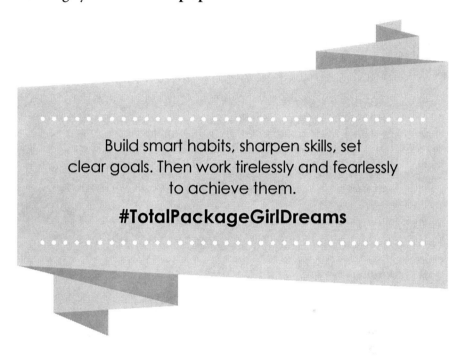

Build smart habits, sharpen skills, set clear goals. Then work tirelessly and fearlessly to achieve them.
#TotalPackageGirlDreams

 **Quiet Time**

Life gets busy, and sometimes you just need to quiet your brain. Spend time doing absolutely nothing once in a while. Turn off all technology as often as possible. Lay on your bed and stare at the ceiling. (See the upcoming **#TotalPackageSpirit** Plan section for further ideas.) Sit and ponder what you did that day or what you want to do tomorrow. Daydream. Allow yourself time to recharge your mind from your busy days. Enjoy your alone time.

Academic Excellence

Work hard for good grades. This will position you for success in high school, college, post-college, and your career. When you push yourself and aim high academically, you set yourself up for great opportunities. Do you have an academic dream? If not, it's time to set one. Ask yourself questions like the following:

* *What is my current GPA?*

* *How do I want to perform on academic tests?*

* *What college or grad school would I like to attend? How do I get there?*

* *What grade point average do I need to graduate with to get into my dream school?*

* *What career path will I explore?*

If your dream is to attend a certain university, do you know what the admissions process is? If you want to be an engineer for a large corporation, do you know the steps it will take to get you there? You may not have thought about these things yet in your life (or maybe you have) and they can seem overwhelming at first, but **#RightNow** is the time to get solid scores and grades, and position yourself for future success. Achieving excellence early in life can open up greater opportunities for your future. Here is an education and academic checklist:

 What is my academic dream? My major/minor? What honors classes and clubs will I join that help build my future dreams?

✅ *What academic tests will I take and what scores would I like to attain? How (specifically) will I reach my pinnacle on these tests?*

✅ *What school(s) do I want to attend? What does it take to go there?*

✅ *What is my GPA? Am I truly doing my best in school? If not, how can I improve?*

✅ *What career path am I pursuing? Am I basing this on my talents, loves, and academic excellence? How can I position myself today for tomorrow's success?*

⭐ Leadership Strategy

Not only does participating in leadership activities position you for reaching your dreams, but it also prepares you to excel in future initiatives in your life. Join a club, organization, or team. Get and stay involved in a sport, hobby, or area of interest so you remain active and involved. While doing so, challenge yourself to step up and be the leader or an officer of that group. If you don't feel you are quite ready for that, ask the coach, advisor or group leader to give you some tips on being a better leader. Communities have youth, young adult leadership, and young professional organizations, so research what is available in your area. You also can visit **TotalPackageGirl.com/brain** and sign up for online professional development courses to sharpen your leadership skills.

 **Time Management**

People budget their money—how much they spend, how much they save. What about doing a budget for your *time*? Let's face it: time is precious, and it seems like you run out of time just when you were getting things done. Here's a sample of how to get smart with your time by budgeting it wisely. Yours will vary, so you can do the math for your own **time budget**:

One day:	24 hours
Sleep (hopefully!):	-9 hours
School & Homework:	-9 hours
Exercise & Activities:	-2 hours
Travel time:	-1 hour
Meal times:	-1 hour
TIME LEFT:	**2 HOURS**

Summertime and winter vacation are great times to begin a new hobby, to get good sleep, to sharpen your skills in sports and activities, to hang out with your TruBlues, to travel, to serve a community cause, to reach out, and to help those in need.

Ask: "How can I get physical, broaden my intellectual horizons, explore new spirit-enriching activities? How can I maximize my time left, those two important hours, and make great use of my time?"

TOTAL PACKAGE GIRL ACTIVITY:
Those Two Hours

What do you do with the spare time you have—those two important hours left in your day? Do you maximize them by doing productive things, or do you spend them on unproductive or unhealthy things? A great way to spend your extra time is to do activities that help others or that support your dreams and goals.

My Time Budget:
Write the amount of hours you spend per day in each box.

SLEEP	SCHOOL & HOMEWORK	EXERCISE & ACTIVITIES	TRAVEL TIME
☐	☐	☐	☐

MEALTIMES	OTHER	TIME LEFT
☐	☐	☐

How do I spend my "time left?"

How can I use that time more wisely to help others or to support my dreams and goals?

BRAIN PLAN

 **Money Plan**

It's important in life to begin thinking about your money situation and how to save for your future. Establishing good habits like saving your birthday or holiday money in an account **#RightNow** is the first step. Ask yourself questions like:

- *How much money do I currently have or earn? What is my primary way to earn money?*

- *Would I like to earn more and if so, how will I do that?*

- *Am I a saver or a spender?*

- *How much money would I like to make?*

- *What upcoming purchases do I have (e.g., a car, a professional suit, a phone)?*

Start planning some financial dreams and **#TPJournalIt**. Begin researching ways to invest your money. Read about career opportunities that match your money plan and vice versa.

 Scan this QR code to check out our Total Package Girl Money Series at **TotalPackageGirl.com** for a twelve-week intro course on how to manage your money.

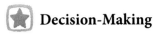 **Decision-Making**

Your **#TotalPackageBrain** Plan requires smart decision-making to prepare and position you for many great, fun future opportunities. Smart decision-making leads to exciting things like going to an awesome college, establishing a successful career, and building a happier life. Every chance you get, make choices based on your Total Package Girl path to help you reach your dreams.

Our deepest fear is not that we are inadequate;
our deepest fear is that
we are powerful beyond measure.
—*Marianne Williamson*

Part Three of Your Master Plan Is Your #TotalPackageSpirit Plan

You are on the path to becoming an amazing Total Package Girl for life. You now have the first two parts of your Total Package Master Plan: the *Body Plan* and *Brain Plan*. Now it's time to enrich that fabulous inner Total Package Girl with a *Spirit Plan*. Why a Spirit Plan? To feel happy and more fulfilled, grounded, and loved as you go through life. And, of course, to have fun and let your spirit soar with peace, gratitude, and love. **#TrueYou**

When you activate your **#TotalPackageSpirit** Plan, you learn to take care of and love your inner you—and it shows. You discover and reignite your spirit and may actually begin to feel lighter, as if your spirit is soaring. You may feel like a happier, more loving person, with amazing dreams. And guess what? Others may discover and love themselves more by seeing your example!

Sacrifice for Others

The first component of your plan is to act unselfishly. Give up your seat, let someone go before you in line, give someone a small gift to say thanks. Look for ways to be a more loving person. Think: *How can I be super-kind in my world? What can I sacrifice today to help another person?*

Strategy for Excellence

Do the right thing when no one is looking. Ever drop litter on the ground and not want to pick it up because no one saw you drop it? Pick it up anyway. Ever see someone drop change all over the floor at the local coffee house and try to pick it up alone? Help out. Even when no one asks you to, just do it out of your own spirit of excellence.

Sometimes it takes extra effort on your part, but it's worth it. You will make someone's day brighter or the earth a little greener. You may make a difference in the life of someone and not even know it. How awesome is that! Keeping your eyes open to the needs of others around you is how excellence starts.

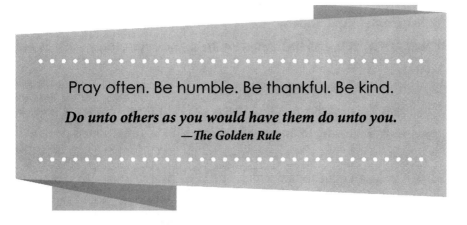

Pray often. Be humble. Be thankful. Be kind.

Do unto others as you would have them do unto you.
—*The Golden Rule*

 Inner Peace

If you went through life always knowing exactly what to do and never making a mistake, your life would be perfect, right? Well, that will never happen because we all make mistakes and life isn't perfect, nor is it easy. If it were, when would we learn and grow?

You can, however, find inner peace in life by living lovingly and honestly. Find inner peace by not lying, cheating, stealing, backstabbing, or acting mean toward others. If you can get up in the morning, look at yourself in the mirror, and know that you live an honest life by treating others fairly, lovingly, and with respect, you will find peace. And at night, if you can lay your head on your pillow and feel that you did your best that day, you also will feel peace inside.

Smart Relationships

Yes, be a bit choosy with your friends. Choose nice over mean. You know how to identify your TruBlues and how to spot anti-TruBlues who disguise themselves as TruBlues. Do not allow your spirit to be deflated by hanging around with someone who repeatedly tears you down or makes fun of you, has bad behavior, or is mean to others. That is not healthy.

Switch out the negative people in your life with positive ones whenever possible. By choosing loving, positive, kind, good-intentioned people to be in your world, you can love more easily and nurture a happy spirit. Also, if you can help soften a mean person's heart, do it with a random act of kindness. That's a true act of love.

Stress Reduction

To keep your spirit soaring and lower your stress, release, like a butterfly, things that are out of your control. As a Total Package Girl, work hard on *not* worrying. Train your mind not to worry about those things you cannot control, like the weather, or what actions others take or words they speak. Remember, take action when you are worried so you feel you are making progress in the situation.

Turn away from worry by looking at the bright side of the situation. If there is someone in your life who is contributing to your stress, assess who it is, how important that relationship is to you, and how you will handle it in the future.

 Self-Trust

Whether or not you go to church, temple, or another place of worship, you can build your spiritual muscle and your faith. Sometimes doubt in your own talents and abilities creeps in—perhaps someone put doubt into your mind that you weren't good enough for something, or perhaps you lost confidence due to a mistake or failure. When you build your spiritual muscle, you feel grounded, and you gain confidence in your beauty and your positive attributes, which leads you right back to your Total Package Girl path. Trust, don't doubt, your abilities. You are amazing inside and out.

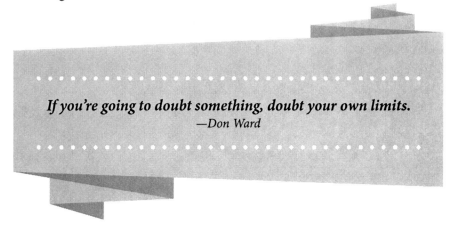

If you're going to doubt something, doubt your own limits.
—Don Ward

SPIRIT PLAN

Here are some ways to eliminate doubt and develop your strong spiritual muscle:

- ✅ *Spend time doing good things for other people—help an elderly person with housework, rake leaves for your neighbor, assist a disabled person.*

- ✅ *Pray and be thankful for all you have.*

- ✅ *Smile more, and mean it.*

- ✅ *Show gratitude and appreciation to those who've helped you along the way—just a simple verbal "thank you" or note will do. A hug works too.*

- ✅ *Keep a spiritual quotation book and/or this book on your nightstand and read it nightly.*

- ✅ *#TPJournalIt.*

- ✅ *Revisit your Total Package Girl Secret Weapons, past successes, fun events, your talents and your loves, to remember the beautiful, amazing, confident you.*

- ✅ *Other ideas? Write them here.*

Faith (n.)

Trust, confidence, optimism, hope.

*The teenager put her **faith** in her Total Package Girl Master Plan and she became her own uniquely beautiful piece of art.*

 Personal Growth and Development

Someone once said that we are either in a challenge, just finishing a challenge, or soon to be in one. As you've learned, life will give you tests—those absolute realities you cannot control. If something keeps repeatedly challenging you or is bothering you, it's a test, a thorn in your side, but also a growth opportunity. It's showing you who you really are based on how you are handling it. Are you going to pass the test and get beyond the thorn, or are you going to let it keep driving you crazy and bothering you as a lifelong challenge? One of your biggest challenges as a Total Package Girl is to figure out how you can conquer, live through, and grow in a positive way from life's tests.

It may be a person, a past situation, or hurt feelings that are causing you to be challenged. If this test continues, picture yourself as a hurdler running down a track; the hurdle is your test. As you approach the hurdle, you have choices:

a) *Stop at the hurdle and turn back*

b) *Run around it*

c) *Run head-on toward it and jump over it*

The choice is yours. Will you continue to carry the burden with you and let the hurdle stop you, will you find another way to deal with it and sidestep or ignore the issue, or will you use every bit of power you have and attack it head on? The last option is the most direct way to deal with this particular life test.

Meditation

Meditation is deep thinking, reflection, and cogitation. When it becomes a habit, meditation calms your body and mind and relieves worry. That is why it is such an important component of your Total Package Lifestyle. There are many different ways to meditate:

- *Use deep breathing to calm you down, keep you peaceful, and chill you out.* Inhale slowly and deeply through your nose and exhale through your mouth slowly like you are blowing through a straw. Inhale and exhale four times slowly like that. Do this every time you need to slow down, calm down, or just plain relax.

- *Join a yoga class* to stretch, tone, strengthen, and get peaceful with your body.

- *Pray often,* especially at times of conflict, stress, or when you feel worry coming on. Be specific and ask for what you want in your prayers. Be thankful, too.

- *When you start to worry, think practical, rational, realistic, good thoughts, and focus on things you know are true.*

Relax regularly so stress doesn't creep into your life. Build ten or fifteen minutes into your time budget every day at the same time to develop your meditation habit. Find a chill spot, kick your feet up, grab your favorite blanket and pillow and your snuggly pet, take a deep breath, and just be. You also can practice progressive muscle relaxation where you squeeze certain muscles of your body and then release them and feel the pressure leave your body. For more on this, get the **#TotalPackageSpirit** Plan at **www.TotalPackageGirl.com/spirit**.

 Laughter and Fun

If you are a serious person, laughing doesn't come naturally for you. That means you need to build a habit of laughter. It may even be forced at first, but laughter is a great way to make a tough day better or a good day great. Know what cracks you up and makes you laugh out loud—a joke book, home movies, a funny TV show or app, a silly hobby, a funny friend. Whatever and whoever it is, bring those people and things into your life. Laughter decreases stress, increases feel-good endorphins, and lightens a rough day.

SPIRIT PLAN

Self-Love and Self-Respect

Your spirit becomes stronger when you love yourself. Do you love you? If you cannot say a resounding "yes" yet, make it your top goal to fall in love with yourself—to **#LoveYouSomeYou,** as in Total Package Girl Secret Weapon #3. When you respect and love yourself by treating yourself in healthy ways, you feel calmer, more energized, and happier. You can take the next step confidently. When you are spiritually happy, goals become clearer and dreams become closer to reality. You're living true to yourself.

Every day, practice **#MeMantras,** telling yourself how beautiful, valuable, and wonderful you are. Do a good deed, honor your Body, Brain, and Spirit, and practice the steps in your **#TotalPackageSpirit** Plan throughout the day. Keep your eyes open, because good things will be all around you if you are looking. Respect all that you are.

TOTAL PACKAGE GIRL ACTION: Do One Kind Thing

On your next birthday, or for a New Year's resolution, or just because, commit to doing one new thing or one kind thing every single day. Record your actions and see how long you can keep them going. For example, help an elderly person carry groceries, open the door for someone, give to a worthy cause like a food pantry or homeless shelter, or buy the person behind you in line a coffee. What other things can you do every single day to make someone's day brighter?

Your Dreams and Success

In Total Package Girl terms, success is something you achieve based on your own dreams, ideas, loves, and accomplishments. You may consider it a success—for example, when you've overcome a challenge like learning to walk again after a serious accident and months of physical therapy. Success might be when you've conquered a fear or gotten into the school or company you've always wanted to. Success stems from your spirit and your drive, from personal struggles and triumphs, from standards you set for yourself. Each person has her own definition of success, and no one can determine it for her.

Society suggests that success is fame, beauty, wealth, popularity, high achievement, and/or public recognition. To some, success is the biggest house or the nicest car. To others, success is having loving relationships. Some may equate the latest designer boots to success because perhaps they've never owned designer boots and have saved for years to be able to buy their own brand-new pair.

Insight: Truth is, as you enter new chapters in your life, your success definition may change. The one thing that is constant is that when you activate your Total Package Girl Master Plan, personal life success will follow and your dreams will begin falling into place. That's what living the Total Package Lifestyle is all about.

> No one else can define your dreams or your success. Aim high, trust yourself, and rock your dreams.
> **#UnstoppableTotalPackageGirl**

 TOTAL PACKAGE GIRL ACTIVITY:
Defining My Dreams and My Success

Success means different things to different people. To some, it's achieving dreams like finding a cure for cancer. To others, it's writing a book about a cancer cure. To still others, it's overcoming cancer. Success is by one's own definition.

At this very moment, how do I define my own success and the dreams I wish to achieve?

What steps can I take to activate my dreams and be successful?

Be the Force in Your World

You know *you* are the unstoppable Total Package Girl when you do the following:

- ✓ *Lead by example, and do not follow.*

- ✓ *Look at yourself and know you are beautiful.*

- ✓ *Make a difference in the world ... or to one person.*

- ✓ *Leave everything you do better than you found it.*

- ✓ *Leave footprints that rock your world and others in the world.*

- ✓ *Live your healthy Total Package Girl Body, Brain, Spirit Master Plan every day.*

- ✓ *Keep your eyes open and seize opportunity when it's in front of you.*

- ✓ *Automatically use your Total Package Girl Power Shield to protect yourself and others in need.*

- ✓ *Use your Total Package Girl Secret Weapons to better yourself and the world.*

- ✓ *Trust your smart decisions, actions, words, GPS, self.*

- ✓ *Feel confident and comfortable with who you are, no faking it ... just true-you actions and words.*

- ✓ *Speak positive words about yourself.*

- ✅ *Stop listening to everyone else's voice and hear your own.*

- ✅ *Replace negative energy with positive energy.*

- ✅ *Know your TruBlues and are a TruBlue to others.*

- ✅ *Give of yourself to compassionately help others.*

- ✅ *Have inner peace because you know you are trying and being your best every day.*

- ✅ *Blend your talents with your loves for success.*

- ✅ *Embrace each #RightNow moment, making it better than the last.*

- ✅ *Focus on being awesome, always.*

- ✅ *#LoveMeSomeMe and #jbu.*

· ·

Live (v.)

To be, exist, breathe, walk the earth.

Live every single #RightNow moment to the fullest as the Total Package Girl ... Live savvy, real, smart, successful, and happy.

· ·

Make each moment count. Be the force in your world and leave it more excellent than you found it. *#RightNow*, **Total Package Girl,** *#RightNow.*

That Girl: A Story

That determined little Total Package Girl is all grown up. She never thought she was the Total Package Girl, but turns out, she was. She was kind, stayed strong, and was uniquely beautiful.

She lived through life's absolute realities. She observed or endured fears, bullies, peer pressure, mean girls, tough teachers, poor bosses, and nasty coworkers. She saw the worst of times, felt the pain of illness and death of loved ones, and gained strength through her own survival.

Yet she also experienced the most fabulous of times: laughter, hugs, beauty ... with loving family, with those special people who've evoked brilliant inspiration, and with her most amazing TruBlues. She is humbled by her blessings.

Every day she makes mistakes yet aims to be better. Every day she experiences negative yet craves the positive. Every day she prays to be her best and healthiest self.

The biggest lessons in life she has learned with her eyes wide open—to be a better, kinder, more loving person, and to honor and center her Body, Brain, and Spirit by living the Total Package Lifestyle.

Today, people listen to her voice because she cares deeply about them and works tirelessly and humbly to make a difference in their lives. She loves every **#RightNow** moment of her life and blends her talents with her loves ... and her spirit soars.

Since those early girl experiences, That Girl grew to love and trust herself; to run fearlessly toward her dreams; to be patient and respect timing; to find role models; to challenge herself to be better; to watch and learn from the good and the tough times. She is inspired through learning and has gradually adopted the champion mindset. She speaks up when needed, stays true to herself by using her Power Shield, and remains strong in the face of negativity and meanness. She feels love, success, happiness, gratitude, peace ... **#RightNow**.

She is blessed to be able to speak with and meet people across the globe. She is human ... not perfect. She is a mom, a wife, an award-winning broadcaster, a keynote speaker, an author. She has written a story—her story—to change the world a little bit at a time, to use her voice to help others use theirs, to help others feel and be beautiful, strong, confident, happy, more loving people for life.

She wrote *Total Package Girl* because that's who she'd always prayed about, imagined, and hoped she'd be. In her own way. In her own words. By her own definition.

• •

You are the amazing, unstoppable
Total Package Girl!

Talk to Us! Share with Us!

Download Our App Today

From the App Store

On Google Play

Use the QR codes above or search **Total Package Lifestyle** on your smartphone.

App Store is a service mark of Apple Inc.
Google Play is a trademark of Google Inc.

Visit Our Website

Get our Total Package Professional online courses:
TotalPackageGirl.com/courses

Book Kristi for your next event:
TotalPackageGirl.com/appearances

Nominate a Total Package Girl to be featured on our website:
TotalPackageGirl.com/feature

Share Your Story

Tell us how *Total Package Girl* impacted you or
send Kristi your comments:
Kristi@TotalPackageGirl.com

Join the Total Package Girl Club Today

Sign up online:
TotalPackageGirl.com/club

Check Out Your Master Plan for Body, Brain, and Spirit

TotalPackageGirl.com/body

TotalPackageGirl.com/brain

TotalPackageGirl.com/spirit

Get Social with Total Package Girl

Go to our website to find all of our social hangouts:
TotalPackageGirl.com/social

Total Package Girl Glossary

Absolute Reality (n.)

The real deal, no sugar-coating; the bare-bones stuff; the good with the bad; the pure, no-filter circumstances in life, life happening without rose-colored glasses.

Be (v.)

To live, exist, endure.

Communicate (v.)

To effectively transmit, share and understand thoughts and feelings so that the intended message sent is the message received.

Discern (v.)

To distinguish, detect; to know the difference—between right and wrong, for example—and to determine the right thing to do.

Discover (v.)

To find, bring to light, uncover.

Dream Blocker (n.)

Something (real or imagined) that keeps you from reaching your dreams, from being you. It's an obstacle, a hurdle, a wall, or a behavior that is currently holding you back.

Essence (n.)

The basic, real nature or core of an individual.

Excel (v.)

To shine, be outstanding, exceed.

Exit Strategy (n.)

A plan to get you out of a negative situation.

Faith (n.)

Trust, confidence, optimism, hope.

Fear (n.)

A belief that something is potentially dangerous, unsafe, or painful.

Learn (v.)

To discover, become aware, gain knowledge.

Live (v.)

To be, exist, breathe, walk the earth.

Real (adj.)

Actual, authentic, true, genuine; not fake.

Release (v.)

To set free, unleash.

#RightNow (adj., adv., n.)

To be in the here and now, to acknowledge the precise thought you are thinking, the words you are reading, the feelings you are feeling, the specific smell you are smelling, and the vivid sights and colors you are seeing.

Rock (v.)

To use your power to do what you do in a fun, marvelous, and obvious way.

Secret Weapons (n.)

The inside knowledge, tools, and skills that Total Package Girls own; used as guides for a positive path through life.

Shine (v.)

To glow, sparkle, excel, be brilliant.

Shout-Out (n.)

Public expression of thanks or gratitude.

#TotalPackageGirl (n.)

A girl who is authentic (real), positive, loving, special, kind, and confident in what she does and who she is. Her total package is: her Body, her Brain, *and* her Spirit.

#TotalPackageLifestyle (n.)

A lifetime focus on being fit, healthy, centered, and energetic.

#TruBlue (n.)

A high-quality, trustworthy person who is loyal and steady no matter what; dependable, a personal cheerleader, and a truth-teller. Someone who stands by you, listens without judgment, provides clarity when you are confused, doesn't turn on you, and loves you for you.

Trust (v.)

To rely on, have confidence in, believe in.

Unstoppable (adj.)

Amazing, invincible, awesome, on fire; feelin' it; a force to be reckoned with, incapable of being stopped.

Sources Consulted

Girl Scouts of the USA, Girl Scout Research Institute

Eating Awareness Training by Molly Groger

What Happy Women Know by Dan Baker, PhD and Cathy Greenberg, PhD

Operation: PARENT

Google Dictionary

Harry Potter and the Sorcerer's Stone by J.K. Rowling

The Wizard of Oz by L. Frank Baum

Cleveland Clinic Foundation, Department of Executive Health

National Institute on Media and Family Research

Centers for Disease Control

CPSIA information can be obtained
at www.ICGtesting.com
Printed in the USA
FFOW03n2312110217
32316FF